ALASKA...
In the Wake of the North Star

D1041333

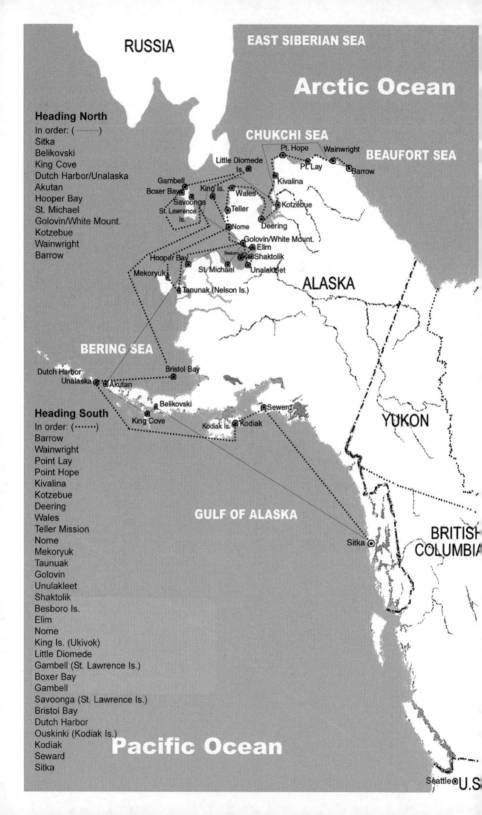

RUSSIA

EAST SIBERIAN SEA

Arctic Ocean

CHUKCHI SEA

BEAUFORT SEA

Pt. Hope
Wainwright
Pt. Lay
Barrow
Little Diomede Is.
Kivalina
Gambell
Boxer Bay
King Is.
Wales
Kotzebue
Savoonga
St. Lawrence Is.
Teller
Deering
Nome
Golovin/White Mount.
Elim
Shaktolik
Besboro Is.
Hooper Bay
St. Michael
Unalakleet
Mekoryuk
Tanunak (Nelson Is.)

ALASKA

Heading North
In order: (———)
Sitka
Belikovski
King Cove
Dutch Harbor/Unalaska
Akutan
Hooper Bay
St. Michael
Golovin/White Mount.
Kotzebue
Wainwright
Barrow

BERING SEA

Bristol Bay
Dutch Harbor
Unalaska
Akutan
Belikovski
Seward
King Cove
Kodiak Is.
Kodiak

YUKON

Heading South
In order: (·········)
Barrow
Wainwright
Point Lay
Point Hope
Kivalina
Kotzebue
Deering
Wales
Teller Mission
Nome
Mekoryuk
Taunuak
Golovin
Unulakleet
Shaktolik
Besboro Is.
Elim
Nome
King Is. (Ukivok)
Little Diomede
Gambell (St. Lawrence Is.)
Boxer Bay
Gambell
Savoonga (St. Lawrence Is.)
Bristol Bay
Dutch Harbor
Ouskinki (Kodiak Is.)
Kodiak
Seward
Sitka

GULF OF ALASKA

BRITISH COLUMBIA

Sitka

Pacific Ocean

Seattle U.S

ALASKA...
In the Wake of the North Star

Loel Burket Shuler

hancock

house

ISBN 0-88839-587-6
Copyright © 2005 Loel Burket Shuler

Cataloging in Publication Data

Shuler, Loel Burket, 1921-
    Alaska...in the wake of the North Star/Loel Burket Schuler

ISBN 0-88839-587-6

1. Shuler, Loel Burket, 1921- — Travel—Alaska. 2. Alaska—
Description and travel. 3. North Star (Supply ship). 4. United States
Maritime Service. 5. Indiansof North America—Alaska—History.
6. Eskimos—Alaska—History. I. Title.

F909.S53 2005   917.9804'4   C2004-904888-0

All rights reserved. No part of this publication may be reproduced, stored
in a retrieval system or transmitted, in any form or by any means, electronic, mechanical, photocopying, recording, or otherwise, without the
prior written permission of Hancock House Publishers.
Printed in South Korea—PACOM

Design and Production: Mia Hancock
Editing: Mary Scott
Art: Rei Muñoz

Published simultaneously in Canada and the United States by

HANCOCK HOUSE PUBLISHERS LTD.
19313 Zero Avenue, Surrey, B.C. V3S 9R9
(604) 538-1114 Fax (604) 538-2262

HANCOCK HOUSE PUBLISHERS
1431 Harrison Avenue, Blaine, WA 98230-5005
(604) 538-1114 Fax (604) 538-2262
Web Site: www.hancockhouse.com *email:* sales@hancockhouse.com

Contents

Acknowledgments 7

Foreword 9

Introduction 12

Hello Alaska 15

Sitka at First Glance 23

USMS North Star II 45

Across the Gulf to the Aleutians 52

Night On Fish River 64

Kotzebue, Crossroads of the North 106

Wainwright to Barrow to North Pole 132

Point Lay, Point Hope and Kivalina 143

Norton Sound "Milk Run" 153

Amazing King Island 172

Homeward Bound 183

Epilogue 192

Afterword 194

Appendix 205

Child of Uncle Sam 214

Glossary of Alaskanisms 218

Suggested Readings 220

Index 221

Our first king salmon catch from on board the Elixir
of Sitka. Author and husband.

For THE STOWAWAY
Whose only memory of her trip will be this book.

"When we Westerners call people 'natives' we implicitly take the cul-
tural color out of our perception of them. We see them as wild animals
infesting the country in which we happen to come across them, as part
of the local flora and fauna and not as men of like passions with our-
selves. So long as we think of them as "natives" we may exterminate
them or, as is more likely today, domesticate them and honestly (per-
haps not altogether mistakenly) believe that we are improving the
breed. But we do not begin to understand them."

— From "The Study of History", by Arnold Toynbee

ACKNOWLEDGMENTS

Septentrion (sept-TEN-tree-on) is a delicious word meaning north. It derives from the Greek root for seven, referring thus to the seven stars of the constellation (Ursa Major) we call the big dipper that points the way to the pole star. In Alaska's night sky one looks straight overhead to see the north star. And it is always there, even when a clouded sky hides its visibility.

There is something emotionally reassuring to the human psyche that one point of light in the firmament remains steady and permanent. To Alaskans that point of light speaks of home, security, and awe. Not surprising then that their flag is a perfect representation of septentrion. And that they love the words to its song, "the great north star with its steady light, o'er land and sea a beacon bright."

In telling my story, I have often referred to the northern native people as Eskimos. This was the habit of the time, the 1950's. Most U.S. citizens of white European extraction knew little or nothing about these amazing people. Many of us, in our ignorance easily lumped together Aleuts, Haida, Tlingit, Tsimshian and Athabascan and called them all Eskimos too. Indeed, when my mother introduced her new granddaughter, born in the Territory of Alaska, to some of her friends in Michigan they quite seriously asked if that made her an Eskimo.

Today's world is smaller, and most of us have learned to be more sensitive and aware. Not all U.S. citizens enjoy being called "Yanks" nor, I imagine, are Canadians especially fond of "Canucks". The northern people of Canada are "Inuit," while the same people in Alaska, also Inuit, sigh with only slight resignation at "Eskimo." All of them know exactly who they really are and what are their mother tongues.

It is more than fifty years too late to thank the people and the institutions who made this extraordinary trip possible. Perhaps that's just as well. They would have been bemused by a "thank you" anyway. They were just doing their jobs. But they welcomed me to tag along and observe and so I hope that those who are still around to read this book will relish the memories. Even more I hope their descendants will read it and take pride in their heritage.

In the world of the present my gratitude and appreciation go to Marilyn Power Scott for her excellent editing skill and for being a good friend; to Mary Scott for patient fine tuning, and more than that for loving what I wrote; to David F. Norman for guiding the manuscript through the mysteries of cyberspace; to my family and friends for their enthusiastic encouragement, without which I might never have returned to this project; especially joyful thanks to Rie Muñoz and her son Juan for graciously sharing Rie's unique art and senior Juan's photographs of a King Island winter; to my dear friend Willy Willoya for sharing memories, feelings, and ideas straight from his heart and his truth and helping me to take a giant step toward understanding another people and their culture; and most of all to David Hancock for making it all come together as a tangible reality.

FOREWORD

The events and experiences described in this book took place more than half a century ago, in 1950. At the time I thought them important not only because of the adventurous nature of the trip but because folks in the South 48 states and the rest of the world we Alaskans call "Outside" knew so little about Alaska. Statehood was looming on the political horizon, and Alaska was about to become a matter of interest. I was laggardly about finishing the manuscript and then laggardly about finding a publisher. My excuse was that the "Stowaway," who turned out to be my daughter, Barbara Rose, was followed in two years by a brother, Mark.

Life went on. I did other things. I left Sitka and Alaska, though I never quite got all the pieces of my heart out of that amazing place. I lived for 40 some years in another beautiful spot, the Monterey Peninsula of California, working with children and classical theater. *Alaska...In the Wake of the North Star*, along with some Alaskan poetry and other bits and pieces, moldered in the bottom of a desk drawer, mostly forgotten.

There is an interesting historical connection between the two places: Monterey was the Spanish capital of California (Alta California) as Sitka was the Russian capital of Alaska. There was even a near joining of Spanish America and Russian America. At the beginning of the nineteenth century, while Napoleon was rampaging through Europe, the Russian Emperor was busily consolidating his holdings in the Americas. Nikolai Rezanof, the dashing young personal emissary of Tsar Alexander had just come south from investigating the loyalty of Baranof in Sitka to the Presidio at San Francisco. He captured the heart of the Spanish Commandant's beautiful daughter, Maria Concepcion Arguella. With the blessings of her father they became betrothed. Although it may well have been a love match there is also clear evidence from Rezanof's papers that he saw the union as a means of adding California to the Russian Empire.

Bizarre as it may seem, had it not been for Rezanof's untimely death California and Alaska both might today be Russian. Maria Concepcion rejected all subsequent offers of marriage and at the age of sixty, after a lifetime devoted to charity and her religion, she entered the new Dominican Convent at Monterey.

Upon such randomly unpredictable events does history often pivot.

Time, happenstance, the advent of the Internet, and the surfacing of some old friends, have brought me back to the story. Somewhat to my surprise I find it still interesting, informative, and entertaining. But now, more importantly, it has become a significant piece of history. The USMS North Star II and her crew are themselves a unique and treasured part of Alaskan history. This story is in many ways as much theirs as it is mine or that of the people and villages of coastal Alaska. That ship, many of its remarkable crew, and some of the most interesting and colorful of the villages no longer exist. All of us who are still around are scarcely recognizable today by a description of us then.

Times have changed in other ways. Most of us have forgotten or never knew how uneasy the Cold War climate made us. I'm also reminded how close we were in 1950 to the experiences of WW II, and how that colored thinking. References to costs and prices are startling. I am surprised to find myself a "figure of history," but that I suppose is what we all are, one way or another. When I was traveling the frozen north, I recognized that changes were happening. I did a good deal of commenting on that fact. I believe I knew it was a transitional moment. But I did not begin to guess the speed and enormity of the changes that were coming. I did not foresee the wiping out of tuberculosis. I did not see the rapidity with which electronic technology would transform the world. I did not foresee that crude oil and pipelines would so significantly change the economy of Alaska, nor what that might mean. I didn't even sense how much air transport and travel would change. That tourists would come in droves to see and experience the last frontier and the new state was not a surprise, but I did not consider just how radically that fact alone could change the landscape. I knew that education was going to cause upheavals. It always does. And I could begin to see that happening already.

But what is most stunning is that for more than a thousand years, Eskimo culture changed almost not at all. And then in less than 50 years it transformed into something so different it takes the breath away. It was going that way when I wrote about it, but who could have dreamed it would go so swiftly, so soon, and so far.

So now, *Alaska...In the Wake of the North Star*, is more important than ever as a chronicle of that moment in time when incredible changes started to bubble. I was privileged to take a close look at an amazing birth and amazingly had the good sense to write about it and photograph it so that none of us has to forget.

INTRODUCTION

An outsider's map of Alaska, even a relatively enlightened outsider, would be similar in distortion to the "Proper Bostonian's Map of the United States." It might include the cities of Anchorage, Juneau, Sitka, and Ketchikan squashed together around the panhandle with a more-or-less ill-defined expanse of tundra above them and Nome and Fairbanks making a sandwich of the North Pole. There is, of course, the tail of the Aleutian Islands trailing out into the Pacific, more related to Asia than America. The whole is liberally doused with ice and snow, dogsleds, and prospectors with picks and packs on their backs and nuggets reflected in their eyes. A few outsiders fortunate enough to have had letters from Alaskan travelers may include somewhere along the coastline a sportsman on a yacht hauling up eighty-pound king salmon with one hand while aiming a 300 magnum at a vicious Kodiak bear with the other. With allowances for a few personal variations, the contours of this mental map are unshakable.

This psychological block on the part of outside friends is a source of never-ending frustration to Alaskans who, with unflagging zeal and optimism, cover reams of stationery with descriptions intended once and for all to implant a realistic picture of the place where they have chosen to live. Yet inevitably they are deflated with such questions as, "But how can blueberry worms survive in such extreme cold?" in response to a glowing description of berry picking stressing the shorts-and-halter sunburn and merely mentioning the worms in passing.

There is an excellent reason for the misconceptions outsiders entertain about Alaska: namely, that Alaskans themselves can't agree on the subject. For this there is also an excellent reason: No part of Alaska is very much at all like any other part. And we all describe what we see from where we sit, and because we each know we are telling the truth, we insist self-righteously that this is the way it is and no other. Small wonder, when one story seemingly refutes another, that outsiders become so confused, they retreat to their squashed mental maps and preconceived notions and will not be budged.

The startling truth is that any outsider could probably safely believe everything ever heard about the Territory, however improbable. Without doubt, it really happened, or it really looked, or it really felt just that way in some place at some time in the 586,000 square miles of extremes that is Alaska. Where the outsider errs is in believing and then assuming, like the blind men and the elephant, that, "This, then, is Alaska!" I have never seen an ice igloo, nor am I to my knowledge acquainted with any Eskimo who has seen an ice igloo. I have a nonspecific notion that somewhere around the northern reaches of the MacKenzie River in Canada, there are nomadic Eskimos who make good winter use of this much-publicized abode. In Kotzebue, miles above the Arctic Circle, where an impressive number of people the world over would swear that the Eskimos live year-round in igloos made of blocks of ice, I heard much gleeful chuckling over the tale of crowds who gathered to watch a white man building a dome-shaped igloo of icy snow for the entertainment

13

of his small daughter. It was the first ice igloo the Eskimos had ever seen, and they were charmed.

There is a vast amount of vitriolic comment made by Alaskans about other Alaskans whose Alaskana gets into print. Invariably they "haven't been here long enough," they "haven't seen the right things," and they "misinterpreted what they saw." They have committed the unpardonable crime of contributing further to the already hopeless morass of misunderstanding about the Territory which it was from 1867 to 1959 before it became the 49th state. While I am as appalled as the next by the astonishing quantity of what seems to me misinformation, I am perfectly certain that on the day when some thorough-going scholar completes the twentieth volume of his encyclopedic study of Alaska, a leathery old sourdough will emerge from a remote spot in the interior and roar across the tundra, "What in God's name makes this cheechako think he can tell anyone about Alaska? He hasn't even been here!" And the sourdough will be as right as the scholar, who will also by that time be a sourdough.

During the three-month period with which this book is principally concerned, I traveled 11,000 fascinating miles by boat with my eyes and my camera lens as wide open as I could keep them. But those 11,000 miles covered only a fraction of Alaska, and three months meant only one northern summer. This I explain carefully, for having lived now a good many years in Alaska I, too, have become sensitive to the rest of the world's misconceptions. I want to contribute my impressions of part of this miraculous land. But I want no one to mistake them for Alaska all and always. Above all I want my fellow Alaskans not to mistake my intentions. I love them dearly. I hope to live with them for the rest of my life. And I do not want them huffing at me.

CHAPTER 1

HELLO ALASKA

We were puttering about making lamps out of driftwood in our basement workshop when Bob casually dropped this bombshell:

"Why don't you make the Barrow trip on the North Star this fall?"

Of all conceivable ways of seeing Alaska; of all conceivable parts of Alaska to see, I could not have envisioned one more exciting than the North Star's Barrow trip up the entire coastline to the most northern point of the North American continent. This is the last and longest of three trips made yearly by the Bureau of Indian Affairs' supply ship. Its duration is three months or more, depending upon weather and complications. The North Star hurries to Pt. Barrow with few stops along the way, taking advantage of the few weeks of summer and absence of the Arctic ice floes, to unload freight supplies for the village. On the return trip, it stops to discharge cargo at villages along the coast, including some of the most remote spots on earth, like King Island, Little Diomede, half mile from the International Date

Line and Siberia, and St. Lawrence Island in the Bering Sea. Why don't I make the Barrow trip indeed!

But I can be casual, too. "Are you going?" I ask, painting my thumb with varnish.

"No, but I thought perhaps you'd like to." This husband of mine sometimes understands me well.

"Oh! Well, I wouldn't want to go alone." I hoped I sounded convincing, for truth to tell, in my imagination, I was already halfway up the Bering Sea and a paroxysmal storm was about to engulf the North Star II in its fury.

"You wouldn't be exactly alone. Hazel and Dr. Sherman are probably going to make the trip."

Hazel Ivy is a nurse-technician in the Mt. Edgecumbe Hospital who began her Alaskan career as nurse for the White Mountain Boarding School in Norton Sound. Dr. Mary Sherman is Associate Professor of Orthopedic Surgery at the University of Chicago. Many of Alaska's crippled children are sent to the University of Chicago hospitals for special treatment, and Dr. Sherman was to make the Barrow trip in an effort to survey at first hand Alaska's orthopedic problems.

Why fence further? Of course, if there were the merest possibility of making the trip, I would leap at it. And I said so.

There followed a spring and summer of preparation, but until four hours before the ship's departure from Mt. Edgecumbe, I would not know for certain that I was to be on it.

The North Star is not by any stretch of imagination operated for benefit of sightseers. Its sole purpose is to serve the outpost stations of the ANS (Alaska Native Service) by providing otherwise unavailable transportation of supplies, students, teachers, and field supervisors. In addition, it is outfitted with a nurse, who is part of the crew, and a sickbay and clinic for transporting patients to and from the hospital and for seeing

16

patients en route and x-raying the chests of the hundreds of natives in the villages it visits.

The Star is a standard-sized freighter recently purchased for the ANS and reconverted to serve its needs. Until its acquisition, the route had been covered for eighteen years by the North Star I, a wooden icebreaker that had made two trips with Admiral Byrd on his Antarctic expeditions, trips on which the present skipper Captain C. H Salenjus served as mate and Cecil C. (Moe) Cole, now first mate of the North Star II, was cabin boy. The old North Star with its romantic history was a dearly loved ship along the Alaska run. But times change. Needs become greater. Eventually the old North Star was too small to carry cargo adequate to the requirements of northern stations, and the smaller gave way to the larger North Star II, and this is how it all came to be!

But you might ask, how did I get to Alaska?   To stateside acquaintances, I was an Alaskan: trail breaker, frontier seeker, and all that goes with it. For my first six months in this lavish land of southeastern Alaska I agreed with them. But there came a time when I sat before a large-scale map of the Territory with my finger marking a spot fifty yards across the ship's channel from Sitka, where I lived in a ridiculously luxurious, almost palatial, ten-room home, and pondered the vast reaches of land pictured northward and westward from my finger. In fact, my finger was so few map miles north of Seattle in comparison to its distance south and east of Point Barrow that I felt peculiarly sheepish about calling myself an Alaskan at all.

I arrived in this almost mythical land by a devious and unsuspecting route, through bright lights, big cities, and one of the more harassing and metropolitan professions, the book-publishing business. After eight relatively successful years as a publisher's sales and promotion manager, I was comfortably certain I had found my niche in life. So certain and so ensnared by civi-lization's metronome chant of "Go! Go! Go!," I neglected to allow for the unpredictable doctor husband to whom I had pledged first allegiance some years before. Happily I had fol-lowed him westward from medical school through internship and residencies, transferring my professional interests from one letterhead to another, and missing altogether the warning hiero-glyphics on the wall. I was visiting my old office in Chicago, about to start the homeward lap of a six-week business tour of the East Coast and Middle West as representative for my Seattle firm, when his letter caught up with me. He had just accepted a position as medical director of an Alaska Native Service hospi-tal in Mt. Edgecumbe, a community, he reported, of 1200 on an island called Japonski across the channel from Sitka, a "city" of 2500. I was stunned. The only rational thought I recall having was that he must have inadvertently omitted a zero from each of his population figures.

He proceeded to Alaska and his new duties while I spent sev-eral months winding up affairs and fulfilling previous commit-ments. Then still in a state of bewildered trauma I sailed from a Seattle dock on the Alaska Steamship Company's vessel Denali, and thus began the insidious process of transforming my entire concept of life in this twentieth century. I was grateful indeed for the four and one-half leisurely days on shipboard. They were scarcely enough to soften the blow of transition from a world where trigger-quick ideas and knowledge of the latest word off the teletype and its import for tomorrow are all important, to a world where the freshest news was ten days old and sifted down to minimal facts. (Sitka at that time had no radio station at all.) And where nobody cared very much anyway. For weeks I felt like a rat in an unfamiliar maze, keyed up with explosive ideas and concerns, and unable to find an opening that would lead me into the proper compartment for putting them to use.

Gradually the tension of the competitive world oozed out until a morning of sunshine came when I could absorb the majesty of mountains, trees, and sea and consider this land of Alaska, its people, its problems, and the wonder of being so glad to be here. This was the beginning of my brief period of feeling that I was an Alaskan, before I got to map studying. When I was still awed by the return address I typed onto letters.

I considered the boarding school of 600 Alaskan Indian, Aleut, and Eskimo high-school students, which, with the tuberculosis sanitarium and orthopedic hospital, comprised the raison d'etre for this island community. When I discovered that the pretty but uncommunicative Athabascan girl, a freshman in the school, who came to help me clean house on Saturday mornings, did not know that cleaning the bathroom included scouring the tub, I realized with a jolt that almost none of these 600 students and 400 patients had either seen or imagined a bathtub before they arrived in Mt. Edgecumbe. And, if this was so of bathtubs, then what other facets of Western culture that people like me started taking for granted the day we were born, were only just coming within the imaginative ken of these children from the north.

Repeatedly I was amazed that my pint-sized Toy Manchester dog, 8 inches high and 14 inches long, with her full-sized bark, would terrorize the students. Pixie was capable of startling anyone with her abrupt and noisy approaches. But the startle reaction customarily turned to amusement at her absurd size. Not so, though, with these students. They gave her a wide and wary berth. And their fearful faces did not reflect her benign cuteness. To them a dog was a dog, and a wildly barking on-coming dog was, from a lifetime of habit, a danger to get as far away from as quickly as possible. Gradually, as one by one they became acquainted with Pixie and discovered that she was a friendly, affectionate little creature who responded alertly to commands other than mush, gee, and haw, she began to be a source of wonder and delight. Once she had the for a dog, degrading-experience of portraying "Pussy-in-the-Well," for a dramatization of nursery rhymes performed by the sophomore class. After the show she was so feted and pampered and stuffed with pastries that I could scarcely live with her superiority complex for weeks.

Pixie, like bathtubs, was a new, undreamed-of product of the "outside" world.

Now, there are bathtubs in Sitka, and bathtubs in Ketchikan, and bathtubs in Juneau, and bathtubs in Anchorage, Fairbanks and other northern communities. There are in fact so many bathtubs and other accessories of modern living in these metropolitan centers that, second only to its spectacular beauty, the thing that dazzles Alaska's summer tourists in the present era is how much like home and how unlike a gold rush are the cities where the boat docks or the DC-4 plane lands. Obviously the young people of Mt. Edgecumbe did not come from these cities of familiar names. So I began my map studying.

"Where is your home?" I would ask.

"Chitina, Chikaloon, Egekik, Kivalina, Shagluk, Point Lay, Akutan, Mekoryuk, Golovin, Elephant Point, Alitak, Elim," came the unenlightening answers.

I would rush to the map trying to remember the strange name long enough to locate it. Mostly I couldn't remember it that long, for unless you know precisely where you are headed, the map of Alaska is immense and bewildering.

I began to sense that I could no more piece together a mental image of the land and circumstances that had bred these young people than they, in their home villages of the exotic names, could accurately visualize a life containing bathtubs and Pixies. There came the feeling that there was something remarkable about their adaptability to such alien circumstance and ideology.

For the atmosphere of Edgecumbe Vocational School is that

20

of any boarding school campus. There are school dances, competitive sports, a uniformed marching band, assembly programs, a jukebox canteen, and strolling couples. True, the couples do their strolling along an abandoned air strip at the edge of a channel busy with ocean-going vessels and seaplanes. The canteen is referred to as Ship's Stores. The basketball games are played in a gigantic hangar partially converted to a gymnasium. They still for the most part have never seen trains, four-lane highways, skyscrapers, football games, big department stores, television, ballet theater, opera, or legitimate theater. But their minds are occupied by the same lessons and extracurricular activities that occupy students everywhere. It is not surprising if they sometimes stumble in their learning for lack of knowledge of a fact so obvious to the teacher that he or she has neglected to mention it. It is surprising that in so short a time they manage to achieve the universality of students with equilibrium.

As soon as I emerged from my newcomer's daze enough to be a little productive, I undertook the announcing and tape-recording of a series of radio programs sponsored by the Alaska Crippled Children's Association, originating in the Orthopedic Hospital. Since that year had seen the inauguration of a program of teaching in the hospital, most of our broadcasts were conducted in the jury-rigged schoolroom with the children in casts, braces, and traction. A majority of the children were tiny tots between the ages of 5 and 10. The classrooms had opened an entirely new horizon of fascination for them. Partly, of course, because it made a break in the monotony of enforced inactivity, but chiefly because they possessed an inherent curiosity and eagerness to learn and to do.

Watching their metamorphosis from sullen-looking gnomes with an inarticulate suspicion of my microphone and me to downright stage struck kids who clamored from their beds whenever I appeared on the wards, "Make my voice, Mrs. Shuler!

Make my voice!" was inspiring and entertaining. But it led to another train of thought.

Here were more children from the faraway place names and the different culture. These had come to Mt. Edgecumbe not to learn but through someone's concern for their impaired and diseased limbs. They were not here primarily to be taught but to be healed and sent home. Many were so young on arrival that their memories did not go back beyond hospital life. They talked about home with eagerness, but with the same eagerness they talked about trains, cows, and elephants, and one had no more reality than the other. Furthermore, they might do their talking with a Boston ah, a southern drawl, or a Hoosier twang depending on what part of the country their favorite nurse called home. Strange indeed must be the occasion called homecoming for these little ones.

My letters to stateside friends with glowing reports of scenic splendor, boating, fishing, hunting and exploring became thinner and thinner as I grew aware that South Eastern Alaska, wondrous though it surely was, was not Alaska. If my friends believed my letters they must be revising their images of Alaska drastically. It was becoming God's chosen land with a climate of year-round mildness, more rain than snow, and more sunshine than rain, where everyone lived the good life, fishing from five till midnight in broad daylight from his or her own boat and practically in his own backyard, and where the best of civilization existed in abundance and the worst was magically absent. Although this seemed true to me, what did I really know of Alaska?

I wanted to see some portion of those hundreds of thousands of square miles northward and westward.

CHAPTER 2

Sitka at First Glance

A glimpse of Sitka, Mt. Edgecumbe, and surroundings, where my Alaskan peregrinations began, is important to set the scene. I return to my arrival in 1949 and first few months in Alaska to describe this now-familiar place as I saw it then. First impressions, while not always accurate, have a wide-eyed approach to detail that can never quite be duplicated once everything becomes familiar. And this is a book about first impressions. When I reread letters and notes I wrote at that time, I discover information that long association has made me take for granted to the point of forgetting. Or I'm amused at the credulous newcomer. But if you had followed in my footsteps, I think this is the way it would have looked to you, too. I begin on the Alaska Steamship Company's Denali sailing from Seattle to Sitka.

Denali, Oct. 24, 1949
Third Day out of Seattle
There was some roughness when we entered Queen Charlotte Sound, where the Gulf Stream comes in from the open sea.

Passengers disappeared like mice scampering into their holes for the long afternoon.

At nightfall I visited the bridge to meet the Captain and look at the radar screen and navigation charts. It was a thick, dark night making the radar essential and more impressive than it might have been at another time. The screen is about a foot and a half in diameter and can be adjusted to show a radius of from one to ten miles. It has been installed on the Denali and all the other Alaska Steam Ships for about two years at an initial expense of $12,000 per installation. Before radar's invention navigation in these waters must have been hazardous indeed. This Inside Passage as seen on charts is truly a maze. In my land-lubber ignorance I had assumed that Inside Passage meant going up Hecate Strait from Queen Charlotte Sound in fairly open water. Not so! In truth it winds around through narrow channels not even shown on any but the largest charts and the slightest miscue might head a ship straight for a hidden rock.

Denali, by the way, means "Mountain of the Sun" and is the Athabaskan Indian name for the mountain we have so prosaically called Mt. McKinley. The ship Denali unlike the other Alaska Steamships, which are one or the other, is half freighter and half passenger ship.

This morning around 10 a.m. we passed into Alaskan waters. The dividing line is somewhere near Annette Island, a Metlakatla Tsimshian native reservation with perhaps 1000 inhabitants. On one flat side of this island, which is actually a mountain, the CAA (Civil Aeronautics Association) operates an airstrip used as a refueling station and servicing about ten flights daily, as well as not infrequent emergency landings. There is even overnight accommodation for passengers stranded by the unpredictable weather. The Metlakatlans are a fiercely proud and private tribe notable for their red hair. They are also an unusually affluent tribe, having made most of their original money from canneries. They now carry on a lucrative business in oil as a direct result of the airstrip. Even so they exact an exaggerated sum for the lease using as their reason that it has ruined their hunting grounds. Although air traffic may indeed inhibit hunting, the CAA considers this a feeble excuse since the Metlakatlans have long since ceased to hunt as a livelihood.

Once in Alaskan waters the scenery becomes progressively more beautiful. At 1:30 this afternoon we made our first stop at Ketchikan for two hours, time enough to wander the streets and absorb my first view and impression of an Alaskan city. To me the most striking thing was the frontier look. Unpaved streets with plank sidewalks, wooden buildings with rococo fronts, and, of course, the whole town built straight up the side of a mountain so that from the dock all the houses and buildings are visible. It has the look of a frontier novel come to life.

There are incongruities galore. Mingled in this frontier architecture and atmosphere are modern concrete buildings of as many as five or six stories. Ketchikan's new federal building is a beauty. The people are as incongruous as the structures. Natives and hard-bitten characters lounge about mixed with svelte looking women downtown for an afternoon of shopping.

As might be expected I gravitated at once to the bookstore where I spent a half hour chatting with three charming middle-aged women one of whom was sitting at a desk littered with Publisher's Weekly's and other familiar looking reading matter. (I was only days from my publishing career and still in book promotion mode. At the University of Washington Press we had recently published Viola Garfield's *The Wolf and the Raven,* a study of Alaska totems.) We discussed *The Wolf and the Raven,* its sales and its excellence. They hope to arrange an autographing party for Viola when she is in Ketchikan this winter. Everyone here is much incensed over a book by a man named Hilcher from Fairbanks, titled *Alaska Now.* He has not described the major Alaskan cities to the satisfaction of their residents. His goose is really cooked by the fact that he gave gentler treatment to Fairbanks than to the rest.

Pixie in Ketchikan had the time of her life. She was over-joyed to get off the boat. Sensing that we had arrived somewhere she was champing at the bit when I went down the hatch to get her. She pulled me up and out onto the gangplank wild with happiness and barking joyously in all directions. She had only barked once since leaving Seattle. That was at the Captain when she was up on deck and out-of-bounds for dogs. Pixie has no respect for rank or for self preservation. During our stroll about the town she eagerly investigated every new sight and smell. Also in Ketchikan as elsewhere she became at once a center of attention. Everyone stopped to talk with her and pet her and small children trailed us up one block and down another.

Petersburg tomorrow at 4:00 a.m. Leave at 6:00 a.m. Juneau at 2:00 p.m. And Sitka at 7:00 or 8:00 Wednesday morning. From Sitka the Denali goes on to Seward, entirely outside and a rough trip at this time of the year, then South via all the same stops to Seattle. Most of the passengers are either moving to Alaska or returning home. There is just one seating for meals, which incidentally are superb.

There was a whale sighting yesterday. And the constant wheeling of the seagulls is a source of hypnotic fascination. Curious looking black ducks with long necks follow us continuously and dive for food. The sailors call them Hell Divers.

Denali between Juneau and Sitka
October 25, 1949
Much of last night I spent on deck, bitter cold but fascinated. Somehow a ship going places at night seems ever so much more exotic than in the daytime. I waited until 2:00 a.m. to watch us navigate the Wrangell Narrows, a series of twists and turns

around many small islands. It must be run at high tide and so for several hours it was necessary to kill time in order to hit the passage just right. Time killing comprised various maneuvers sometimes going in circles. It was interestingly confusing to know where we were at any given moment.

The Narrows itself is marked with red and green lights between which the ship picks its way. Green is starboard (right) and red is port (left). A mnemonic for this is "red port wine." It's a bit like a slalom run on a ski slope. I'm told that in the daytime one can see houses on each of the islands and people out working in their yards. It is supposedly possible to reach out and touch the trees along either shore. But in the darkness only the red and green lights are visible. No one else was on deck. I am apparently the only foolhardy passenger. At 4:00 a.m. we docked at Petersburg where my cabin mate disembarked causing some commotion. As a result I slept in until 11:00 missing breakfast.

By this time the scenery had undergone another change and was becoming more breath taking by the moment. Snow covered peaks on either side were, in spite of the low-hanging clouds, an inspiring sight. We passed a magnificent blue-green glacier that must have been the Taku, responsible for Juneau's far-famed winds. As a result of my laziness, I missed seeing an iceberg that startled everyone. I also missed two more whale sightings.

Not long after lunch, long enough though to become well chilled by the cold wet rain on deck, we came into Gasteneau Channel and up to the Juneau docks. Here to my surprise my leisurely life as a tourist ended abruptly and I became a VIP. Dr. and Mrs. Googe were waiting on the dock waving a copy of the Juneau newspaper announcing my arrival. The radio also carried this earth-shaking news! I was driven to the Alaska Native Service (ANS) offices and introduced to what seemed like hundreds of people in kaleidoscopic sequence, all of whom welcomed me as a long-expected friend. There was no wandering idly and anonymously about Juneau, and Pixie never even got off the ship.

I did manage to spend some time in the Native Arts and Crafts Shop on the first floor of the ANS building, again talking up Viola's book, and pouring over the small natively carved totem pole replicas and the spruce-root baskets. There was an elegant chief's cane that the artist had to sell after completing because he had been unable to resist the temptation to carve a frog figure on it. He was not entitled by tribal heritage to use the frog. Criticism rained down on him so ferociously he was forced to dispose of it. So now it's on display, not for sale, in the shop.

Juneau was as wet and cold as its reputation, but withal an interesting city. The Baranof Hotel has an air of opulence. Most appealing are the paintings hanging on the walls of the lobby and dining halls. The famous Sidney Lawrence painting of Mt. McKinley that covers one whole wall is so glorious I could sit for hours gazing at it. Somehow he achieved a phosphorescent sunset glow that seems alive.

So far nothing in Alaska has been a disappointment, not even the weather.

October 26, 1949

At 7:30 AM the Denali entered Sitka Sound. Experiencing my first case of channel fever, I'd slept little during the night. Earlier in the evening, I saw that the steward had battened down my porthole. Because the stateroom overheated quickly, I reopened it. Later he stopped me in the companionway and explained that we were due for rough weather in the night and unless I securely closed the porthole, my room could be flooded.

I followed instructions, though they seemed ridiculously overcautious. But after tossing and turning in the stuffiness until two o'clock, I decided to open the porthole just long enough to let in one good gust of fresh air. We were slipping along in such peaceful moonlit water that I could not bring myself to screw it down tightly again before falling asleep. About three o'clock in the morning I was rudely awakened by a sudden lurch and what seemed an ocean of frigid salt water pouring into my face. Needless to say I scrambled to secure the porthole. For three hours, we pitched and tossed, and things crashed to the floor despite my efforts to anchor anything movable. I wondered about landlubber Pixie down in the hold.

At a little past seven, I woke again to a serene ocean and hastened to get dressed and out on deck to watch the entrance to Sitka. None too soon, either! We were already approaching Japonski Island, which I recognized at once by the dominating presence of the new five-story hospital I had seen in an architect's sketch in the Juneau ANS offices. The community of Mt. Edgecumbe is rather impressive from that north-channel approach, even in semidarkness and rain. Sitka comes out second best because all that is visible is the fishing floats and docks along the waterfront. In that early morning dim light, it was overshadowed. This is not to belittle Sitka. It is beautiful against a backdrop of snowcapped mountains. One stunning peak to the south has a natural cross of snow at its pinnacle, not surprisingly it is named Cross Mountain.

It was still dark and drizzling a fine rain as the Denali approached Sitka. I haunted the island side of the deck, the starboard side, striving to distinguish every possible detail of my new home and was offended by a ship's officer who stalked past me several times reiterating officiously, "Port landing! Port landing!" Was he suggesting that this tourist couldn't even distinguish the interesting side of the channel?

Inching up to the dock and making fast seemed a painfully slow process to me, longing to see a husband after four months of separation. In the dim light I could see only blurs on the dock for nearly twenty minutes of snail-pace approach. (By this time

I'd obligingly gravitated to the port side.) Eventually our lines were heaved to the dock, but we were still another exasperating twenty minutes pulling over in troublesome wind and current. By now I could distinguish faces on the dock, and Bob's was not among them. My enthusiasm was punctured and deflated. I nearly went below to eat breakfast as less eager passengers were doing. However, when we were three quarters of the way through the docking maneuver, one of the little shore boats came putting around the Denali's prow, and there he was. From then on for hours life was a confusion of introductions, baggage, nurses, attendants, dogs, boat rides, automobile rides, and kaleidoscopic sights. My arrival alone would have been sufficiently disorganized with all the paraphernalia I had in tow, but added to that were some fifteen other passengers arriving to new jobs at the school and hospital. They were as excited and bewildered as I was. They needed to be greeted, introduced into proper channels, and made to feel at ease and at home. In the midst of the disorder, I kept having glimpses of the once familiar person of my husband who now was unaccountably master of this chaotic situation, which, to judge from his behavior was not in the least unusual. It was afternoon before we had a chance to say more than "hello." It was late evening before we were disentangled from people and events. By then I was too dazed to do more than stammer a few inarticulate sentences and fall into bed.

The next morning I began making the acquaintance of my new home, and there was much to learn about it. The Mt. Edgecumbe installation itself is not a thing of beauty despite its wild and appealing surroundings. It was built by the Navy during the war and has the utilitarian look of a military base. In 1947 it was abandoned because of numerous impracticalities and turned over to the ANS for its present use. Growth of the complex was so tremendous and so rapid that it soon became the main and largest operation of the ANS. But since there was nothing here prior to the war and only the Navy during the war, no current material on Alaska gives it more than scant mention. Maps give it none at all.

To build its installation, the Navy leveled off steep hills and scraped them into the Sound, creating causeways between the larger island, Japonski, undoubtedly named because of Mt. Edgecumbe's resemblance to Mt. Fuji, and several small adjacent ones bringing Sitka and Japonski Island closer together. The narrow span of water between Sitka and Mt. Edgecumbe can be crossed in three minutes by the Navy's old shore boats. The community is named after the perfect cone-shaped volcanic peak located on Kruzof Island some miles southeast of Sitka and a hallmark for both towns.

Housing on the island, thanks to its armed forces heritage, creates the semblance of a hierarchy. There are four large and lavish houses occupied by the Island's administrator, the school superintendent, the orthopedic surgeon, and the medical director. These were built to house the base's commanding officers and are still referred to as the MOQ-Master Officers' Quarters. Down the road apiece is a series of twelve duplexes called the JOQ, Junior Officers' Quarters. These now house staff doctors and department heads. Next in line is the BOQ, Bachelor Officers' Quarters, also known as The Club, where unmarried nurses and teachers live. The rest of the 1,200 people who are not patients or students are housed all over the Island, making use of remodeled navy barracks and other structures. There is a neighborhood called Millerville, another called Charcoal Island, and obscurely, one called Hollywood. A section housing CAA (Civil Aeronautics Authority) personnel is Iggorote Village. For the most part, these are medium-sized houses and apartment units and are as various as the people who live in them. They are reminiscent of the wartime housing projects in all the large cities stateside. Thanks to the rapid expansion, especially of the medical center, there is a constant housing shortage, and construction of new units does not begin to keep pace with the influx of new personnel. Although the difference in quality of the houses is probably no greater than that in any community, it is pointed up by the inescapable arbitrary assignment of housing according to professional position. This led one youngster in the school, when asked to define society, to reply, "society: MOQ, JOQ, and BOQ." Since nothing resembling grass grows in the muskeg covering most of the island any landscaping must be done at considerable effort and expense hauling in topsoil from elsewhere by boat. Consequently there are few attractive yards. The MOQ's, of course, have expansive lawns leading down to the water line of the channel.

The island itself, or, more accurately, the group of causeway-connected islands, is an example of the extravagant waste of war. The Navy poured $75,000,000 into the construction of this base before it was abandoned. When they moved out, they left everything helter-skelter and partially wrecked because although arrangements had already been made for the ANS to take over, no one in authority remembered to countermand the standing order to demolish as much as possible to prevent the enemy's benefitting from it. At the last moment, the lush furnishings of the officers' quarters were loaded onto a barge and carted off to Adak, to the disappointment of the first ANS comers, who had been dreaming of thick carpets, rich draperies and telephones in every room

Moving around the island, one sees all manner of weather-spoiled machinery: steam shovels, tanks, tractors, and landing barges. There are dozens of concrete bomb shelters, ammunition vaults, and lookout stations. There are also countless machine-gun nests, networks of tunnels, and barbed wire entanglements. The several huge but weather-beaten hangars are still full of equipment mostly useless. Part of the reason for abandonment was the fact that it was never possible for land planes to come in here, so that the whole building program of concrete airstrip and hangars was sheer waste. Only the tower atop Hangar I is presently used as the CAA operating control tower for incoming and outgoing Sitka flights, all exclusively amphibious. On one of the farthest small islands actually out in the open ocean, where the wind whips across and the water rages, there was once an Army base. All of the barracks are now washed or blown away and half of what was a paved two-lane road is gone. The entire causeway will wash out in a few more years, but now one can still walk out to the end, and an exciting walk it can be, even. in fine weather. Still standing on the far vulnerable end of the causeway is a handsome log structure, a former officer's club, whose construction cost must have been astronomical. There is no way to move it back to the main part of the island and no electricity out to it. Now a total loss, it too will wash away before long.

When one sees these things and imagines by comparison what some of the islands in the Pacific must look like it, brings the devastating economics of war home with impact. While the attempt to make use of these remnants in developing the school and hospital seems on the surface a splendid idea, in actuality, the surplus material that is going into current construction is so impractical for its present use that it is certain to represent ultimate loss in manpower, repair, and general dissatisfaction.

More about the ANS: It is the branch of the Bureau of Indian Affairs that serves the native residents of the Territory of Alaska. In addition to its vocational school and hospitals at Mt. Edgecumbe, it maintains two other boarding schools, one at Wrangell in Southeastern Alaska, for younger orphaned children, and one elementary school for Eskimo children at White Mountain north of Norton Sound. In communities all over the Territory, no matter how remote, where there are twelve or more school-age children with no other school available, the ANS provides teachers and schoolhouses. There are other, though smaller, hospitals at Juneau, Tanana, Kanakanak, Bethel, Kotzebue, and Point Barrow.

At Mt. Edgecumbe the students are representative of literally every part of Alaska. Presumably they start from the 7th grade and go through the 12th. Not infrequently, however, the teacher in a faraway outpost sends a problem child with the notation that he is ready for Mt. Edgecumbe. Examination may disclose that he is at 3rd grade level. In most cases, he can't be sent back for the purely physical reason of lack of transportation, so Edgecumbe teachers have no recourse but to start him from that point.

The biggest problems, though, are the result of the environments that produce the students, environments so alien to our western concepts of education and society that it is well nigh impossible for us even to contemplate how perplexing the abrupt change must be. We might well stop to ponder whether or not it is such a wonderful thing we are doing imposing our civilization on these people. They lived for centuries within their own culture. We have reason to suppose that they lived those centuries successfully and happily, uncomplicated by neuroses and most of the ailments rampant in our society: measles, whooping cough, the common cold, and that great Alaskan bugaboo, tuberculosis. The diseases were "gifts" from the first European men to penetrate the northland and have wreaked havoc here ever since. The neuroses occur when the disruptive aspects of what we try to teach bombards them. Any Alaskan doctor can testify from discouraging experience that when a native Alaskan does develop a neurosis or psychosis, it is likely to be impossible to heal. There is no common ground of reasoning and understanding to provide a starting point for talking it out. Treatment comes to a dead end before it begins. Still, there is a strong and justified argument for educating Alaska's native people: survival of the fittest. There's no evading the fact that Western Culture will ultimately absorb Alaska. Good or bad, it is as inevitable as a steamroller. Those adaptable enough to adjust will be able to make a go of the new ways. We do our best to teach and prepare those who can learn and try not to anguish over what is lost. It's not a pretty picture. There is much they could teach us, but we do not take time to listen. If someday we humans could learn when cultures collide to select the best from each and discard the worst we might see true progress and enrichment for all.

The medical accomplishments of the Native Service are happier to contemplate. When you have cured a sick man or mended a crippled child, you do not have to ask yourself, "Would he be better off if I had left him alone?" It has its gloomy aspect too, for there is so much to do and progress is so slow. Here at Mt. Edgecumbe, the medical aspect is gaining by leaps and bounds. With the completion and filling of the new hospital, the total number of beds available in the TB sanitarium will be 300. Until Mt. Edgecumbe was inaugurated, only one small sanitarium in all of Alaska was actively treating tuberculosis. After Mt. Edgecumbe, there will be still another, larger sanitarium in Anchorage. The orthopedic hospital of 60-odd beds treats almost entirely children. An active volunteer organization, Alaska Crippled Children's Association, supports this work with money, gifts for the children, salaries for teachers, clothing, and, in the Sitka chapter, actual time spent visiting and entertaining the patients. Added to this are 25 general beds, a school clinic, and a regular outpatient clinic. Upwards of 13,000 patients are seen in the combined clinics yearly. Fruitful though this sounds, it is a mere drop in the bucket of Alaska's need.

Most Mt. Edgecumbe residents are employed by the ANS to serve this picture in some way. Though the focus is the school, the hospitals, and their continuous construction and maintenance, the community nature of the island makes the variety of work the same as one would find in any small town-with one exception. There are no shopping facilities. None! This is a nuisance. We must take a shore boat to Sitka for all shopping, even groceries. One does soon become nonchalant, however. You dash over on the 1 o'clock boat, select your groceries at the Cold Storage, and leave them to be delivered to your home. You do any other necessary shopping, chat with friends on the street, have a cup of coffee in the drugstore, and return on the 2:30 or 3:30 boat. You try to avoid the 4:30, which carries Mt. Edgecumbe's children home from Sitka's schools. Catching the 4:30 is like riding a school bus. If the weather is inclement, which is often, you may order groceries by telephone. But there is no running to the corner for a last minute loaf of bread or a pint of ice cream. Planning ahead is crucial.

The first really new fact of life here is boats. Boats are as essential as automobiles are where most of us came from. A day you don't step foot on a boat is a day you hibernated indoors. Going to a party in Sitka on a cold, rainy night is an experience that defies description. Getting up and down the ramps (the tide may be out 10 or 12 feet, making steep angles on the ramps) and in and out of various boats demands agility. Keeping clothes, shoes, and hairdos from becoming hopelessly bedraggled is a feat of magic. We do it, though, daily and nightly with aplomb. I soon took to carrying dress shoes in a bag and avoiding tight skirts.

Perhaps the most intriguing single aspect of Sitka is the Russian Orthodox Church, St. Michael's Cathedral. The church has universal fame since it is the one remaining emblem of the brilliant Baranof regime in Alaska, when Sitka was known as the "Paris of the West Coast." The "Baranof Castle," which occupies a site on a high hill with the most commanding view in the area, is of little historical import now. It is not the original castle, and it has become dilapidated. There is nearly always someone living there. It rents for $1 a month payable to the Department of Agriculture. Tenants supply their own heat and other utilities and, because it is a porous barn of a place, it costs more to heat than rent and utilities combined cost elsewhere. Its difficulty of access makes just the delivery of fuel a major item.

Unlike the castle, St. Michael's is all that any history buff could ask. It also is not the original but was built during the Russian reign when Bishop Innocent returned to the Sitka diocese from his missionary barnstorming in the rest of the Territory. His success in these peregrinations earned him both the honored title and the honored position in Sitka. The present church was completed in 1848 and was the only building to survive the fire that destroyed the castle. The first church had been built in 1799, when Baranof designated Sitka as the Alaska capital and headquarters for the Russian-American Fur Company.

The church was a special pet of the Tsar who once sent a shipload of treasures to glorify it. Sadly, the ship was wrecked on Cape Edgecumbe and nothing recovered. Still between the Tsar, other interested persons in Russia, and the colonists themselves, a truly impressive collection of icons, chalices, crucifixes, tapestries, and miniatures was gathered together in the cathedral. Some of the precious tapestries of unadulterated gold and silver threads were woven by Baranof's daughter, to combat her boredom. The most phenomenal treasure, astonishing to find in such an out-of-the-way corner of the world, is the Sitka Madonna, a painting of Our Lady of Kazen by Vladimir Borovikovsky who, according to Father Sergius, my guide, was a Russian painter comparable to Raphael. The painting's beauty suggests that this is not exaggeration. Icons are almost always adorned with beaten gold and silver, covering most of the painting. Only faces and one hand are left uncovered. The gaudy effect of Russian church art almost blinds a westerner to its intrinsic beauty. In St.

Michael's, the effect is made more absurd by the meager background. The present banning of religion in Soviet Russia made the Orthodox Church an exile, and St. Michael's is so poverty stricken that is impossible to keep it up as an appropriate home for such treasures. The icons, materials of worship, and the great golden doors are magnificent and probably priceless. But Father Sergius showed us two chalice covers of gold and silver threads on green velvet woven by the Princess herself, spreading the display on a warped kitchen table covered with cheap, worn, green and white checked oilcloth.

This particular church's poverty is a little hard to understand in view of the fact that it is the center of a still active missionary program. Every village in the Aleutians has its Russian Orthodox Church, though there are only three or four priests remaining in the Territory. Each parish sends regular tithes to the Sitka Cathedral. Priests live at starvation level and are hard put to subsist at all. The Bishop, however, is apparently a well-to-do though miserly man. His home is reputedly full of more valuable treasures than the church itself, though few people and no one I know have ever been shown through it. True, the Bishop's House belongs to the church, but I once asked an old man of the village and stalwart of the church if the Bishop had a private income. He shrugged his shoulders. Then with a rather sorrowful twinkle in his expressive eyes said, "The Bishop is not a very good Christian, I'm afraid." Father Sergius told me that when he came here from Kodiak, he was given a list of the valuables in the church but found only a fraction of them actually there. His explanation was that "past priests and bishops must have taken them."

From the first, I heard about Father Michael Ossorgin, a young and talented priest who had been in Sitka and had left not long before to live in San Francisco. He was adored in the community, and all were hoping find a way to facilitate his return. Subsistence at St. Michael's was threadbare, and he had been receiving alluring offers from outside. He is a musician. Music, especially concert piano, is his first love. He entered the priesthood originally because of the opportunity it afforded to study music.

Though born in Moscow, he grew up and studied in Paris. Then he was caught by the war and spent years in a German concentration camp, after which he came to Alaska as a displaced person. What I heard about most was the acappella boy's choir he had created from students in the Mt. Edgecumbe School. Sitkans had no adjectives too superlative for this choir. I skeptically reserved judgment. This was, after all, pretty far from discriminating music centers. None the less, it was clear that this man had left behind him an uncommon void.

Fr. Sergius had been called from Kodiak to take Fr. Ossorgin's place. At first I inclined to sympathize with Fr. Sergius, for trying to fill those shoes seemed a thankless task. But Fr. Sergius had known Fr. Ossorgin when he was a small boy in Paris and took a fatherly pride in his success. He, too, wanted Ossorgin back. And Fr. Ossorgin, having had enough of the disquieting effects of metropolitan life, was as eager to return as everyone was to have him. Only material considerations presented obstacles. Finally, the ANS offered him a teaching position and housing on the island to supplement his work in the church, and just before Christmas, he returned. The boys of his choir were at the Alaska Coastal Airlines float to meet him when the plane was due. The plane, however, was 18 hours late, having been forced to overnight in Hoonah. At sundown, the dejected boys trooped home. At the crack of dawn, they were back and resumed their vigil shivering on the float until at last, the Gruman Goose seaplane arrived. Their radiant faces stiff with cold, they sang their favorite, "Dem bones, dem bones, dem dry bones," as Fr. Ossorgin, flowing black hair, beard, and robes, came up the ramp. It was awesome. When at last I heard them sing, I was struck dumb. I don't believe I have ever been more moved. These Aleut, Eskimo, and Indian boys came from the really far reaches of Alaska. They have an evident natural love of music but no previous training. Ossorgin plucks music from them as he would a piano. I'm sure they could enthrall any audience from here to Carnegie Hall.

Alaska has a persuasive tendency to encourage people to resurrect half-forgotten talents, brush off the dust of disuse, and have fun. As a result, a group of us on the Island organized an "orchestra" of musical has-beens (or, wish-they-had-beans,) strictly for our own amusement. After one of our sessions, Fr. Ossorgin and our pianist, who was certainly no has-been, sat down with a volume of two-piano arrangements of Beethoven symphonies. On a single piano, they performed all of the 1st Symphony and the first movement of the Eroica for a spellbound audience. It is less thrilling but perhaps even more intriguing to see Fr. Ossorgin in orthodox clerical vestments, execute a competent jam session on Bumble Boogie, Mule Train, or, I've Got a Lovely Bunch of Coconuts.

Which incongruous train of thought calls this event to mind: On a blizzardy Saturday in early winter, we attended a Hawaiian Luau at the Sitka Elk's club, complete with barbequed pig, coconuts, orchid and carnation leis, and grass skirts, all flown in from Honolulu. On the same night, the House of David basketball team from Benton Harbor, Michigan (which happens to be my home town), played the Alaska Native Brotherhood team on the new gymnasium floor just laid in Hangar 3 by members of the Mt. Edgecumbe Lion's Club. What a small amazing world this is!

A weekend excursion with friends on their 48-foot yacht, Romany III, was my initiation to the wildness and variety of southeastern Alaska. We did not go far, but we might as well have traveled 2000 miles for none of the places we visited looked at all like Sitka and environs. Romany's course was south until we reached an appealing cluster of small islands off the middle of Baranof Island. We prowled over these for hours, skiffing from one to another.

Hunting season had ended the week before, so the rifles we carried were for target practice or the unlikely chance of meeting a brown bear. Though what we would have done in case of such an encounter I have no idea. We climbed to the top of each craggy island to watch the surf pounding against the rocks below and shooting up gigantic spray screens. Hundreds of small gnarled trees with a mossy-vine-covered undergrowth blanketed the rugged terrain. The awkward scrambling over and under the rocks and branches brought out latent mountain goat traits, especially in Pixie, who skipped about delightedly as though she'd been born there. We took care not to go ashore where there was any suspicion of bear, for Pix would have been likely to scare one up and give us a more exciting time than we wished. Presumably the bears mind their own business so long as trespassers mind theirs. But minding her own business is not a Pixie strong point. The picture we made in outdoor clothing and packing rifles was good Alaskan form marred only by Pixie, who couldn't look like a hunting dog no matter how hard she tried. And she did try. She posed like a pointer and sniffed trails like a hound, showing her true canine instincts. Still, she looked like a misplaced pocket model.

Late in the afternoon, we went on to Goddard Hot Springs on Baranof Island. Were it anywhere in the lower states, this would be a thriving resort. Its sulphur hot springs reach a temperature of 146 F. The Dr. Goddard who gave it his name built it into a resort, but it proved so inaccessible that it was finally deserted. There is a rambling hotel and four or five smaller cottages, all heated by pipes circulating hot-spring water through the rooms. There is just one permanent resident, Gus, though Gus had a fisherman crony named Christie with him. These two are isolated except for Christie's troller, Gus's Cris Craft runabout, and occasional visitors like us. Gus cooks in a kitchen designed to feed dozens of paying guests. Gus told us that years before, he had been a chef and later a waiter in Chicago's old Auditorium Hotel (he switched to table waiting when he found there was more money to be made). When the brand new LaSalle Hotel opened, he transferred over to it. The LaSalle's dining room opened for business before construction was complete, and the management brought in branches from the woods to disguise and decorate the uncovered ceiling rafters. Gus the waiter was carving roast duck for a table of customers. To his chagrin, the knife slipped and the duck took off toward the branches. Losing professional poise, Gus exclaimed, "Hell! The godarn duck wants to fly yet!"

He was "godarn" sure he would be fired because "cussing was agin' the godarn rules." But the delighted guests told the headwaiter that Gus was "the best godarn waiter in the place."

Christie, a weathered-looking tough old fisherman, took one look at Pixie and lost his heart. Ignoring Gus's assertion that she was only a "soup-hound," he was determined to lure her into being the first mate of his troller He told her crooningly that she could have fish and beefsteak and he would shoot a deer just for her. She could have cigarettes and coffee, if she liked, but no whiskey. He would teach her to bark every time he landed a fish, and she would have so much fun she would never, never be homesick. I promised Christie that the first puppy Pixie ever had would be that first mate . That will be the most loved and spoiled dog in the world.

Goddard's grounds are abundantly green, and naturally so, not imported landscaping. Gus gave us celery from his garden that was so deliciously sweet and juicy, we ate it ravenously. He gave us cabbages, lettuce, tomatoes, and onions all of a size and quality to please the most discriminating produce merchandiser. This plethora of growing things seems the more remarkable when one has climbed the ridge immediately behind the resort. For here is a stretch of land out of a wild and eerie nightmare - the Burn. It is one of only a few places in Alaska where fire has destroyed timbered area. The soil is all muskeg, southeastern's equivalent of northern tundra. It's sour and spongy and saturated with water even when, as in this instance, it is on a precipitous mountainside. Walking through it is horrid. You don't see the water until you're in it. We kept sinking to the ankles in what looked like solid ground.

Although the burn happened twenty or thirty years ago, moss and coarse grass are all that's grown back. The trees are bleached and beaten by the weather until they are dead white and smooth as driftwood. But they all remain standing where they once grew, their grotesque shapes and color making them a nerve-jangling ghost forest.

Yet the Burn was not the most disconcerting place we found. Coming down from the ridge where charred land and the lush hot springs merged, we entered a jungle of low growth. Long, tenacious branches wore tentacles of hanging moss, like some southern bayou. The treacherous, uneven ground was carpeted with lifeless pale green moss. Sunlight filtering through the branches came from a late afternoon sun that did unorthodox things to colors. It was such an Alice-in-Wonderland world that I could easily believe I was wandering dazed in some schizophrenic fantasy. It was a profound relief to emerge finally from this twilight world to the green freshness around the springs.

Back aboard the Romany after our day in the wilds, each of us had a hot shower. Luxury! We had a dinner of meatloaf, carrots and peas, baked potatoes, fresh celery, hot rolls, and chocolate cake with burnt sugar frosting. We lounged with warm slippers on our no longer wet feet and read a week-old New York Times. We listened to music from South Pacific and the Caesar Franck Symphony and played Canasta until an early and welcome bedtime. Very civilized indeed.

CHAPTER 3

USMS North Star II

Yes. The large freighter North Star II replaced the wooden ice breaker North Star 1 of Antarctic and Arctic fame.and I had varnished my thumb, consolidating my decision to abandon my husband of 8 years and go to learn by experience the real edge of Alaska all the way to Point Barrow.

With an unexpectedness that left me reeling, my desire to see some of the Alaska hinterland wafted out of the realm of desired fantasy into the realm of possibility. This is not the first time in my life that my daydreams have come to sudden and close approximation, but experience never seems to teach me to temper them accordingly.

In her book, *Hearth in the Snow*, Laura Buchan, through the voice of a teacher in one of these isolated spots, described the feeling of connection to the outside world with the arrival of the old North Star gave to those people along the route.

This old familiar motor ship had been used to serve the Alaska Native Service schools, defying stormy seas, whipping winds and dangerous ice packs to deliver cargoes to the loneliest spots on earth. Loaded with food and medical supplies, fuel, textbooks, mail, and equipment of all kinds, she called at schools all the way up the Alaskan coast and her annual visit, interrupted only by the war, was like the arrival of a beloved friend. ...

Each year our village waited anxiously for her call after the radio report came in that she had left Seattle and was on her way north. Finally the night always came when we were able to pick her up as she notified ports to the east and south of us when she would dock.

"She's at Kodiak now," Bill announced one evening on her last run. "Now let's see, if the weather doesn't change she should get here in about eight days."

Each night after that we followed her on her way. Eventually the night came when she signaled us.

"The North Star to Bristol Bay Village, the North Star to Bristol Bay Village," her radio operator "Sparks" called. " Come in Bristol Village."

After that we had only two more days to wait. Keeping in contact with her every few hours, we watched the horizon for her. Suddenly, at one day's dusk, the masts appeared. As we towed her with our eyes, she sailed out of the purple sunset, etching her silhouette against the evening sky. Fourteen miles off shore she anchored outside the sand bar that kept large ships beyond our harbor.

"We'll be in at high tide, at two in the morning, " radioed "Sparks."

Just before two Bill and I climbed into the school truck and went down to the beach to wait, waving lanterns back and forth to guide the ship's launch to a good landing spot. For such ports as ours the North Star carried with her a launch and scow for the delivery of cargo. Heavily loaded with our supplies and members of the crew, the scow rocked sluggishly behind the launch as we watched it crawl over the rough fourteen-mile stretch of water.

Arriving at the beach, the first person off was the Alaska Native Service nurse assigned to the ship. While the nurse and I went back to the schoolhouse to talk shop, the crew unloaded the cargo. Each year the nurse had come to inspect the school, and go over our stock of medical supplies, and check up on health conditions. Sometimes she took one of the village children to an orphanage or another school.

First radioing the ship that the scow was in and the cargo being put ashore, I showed the nurse around the school and picked up from her capable quick mind the solutions to nagging problems. Briskly she chased the cobwebs of anxiety out of the village with an antiseptic sweep. Our rounds completed and the village troubles bandaged, we returned to the beach with pots of coffee and the cookies and cakes I had made the evening before.

The beach was speedily being turned into a supply dump as the crew, the men of the village and Bill all worked furiously at unloading. They raced against the schedule of the sea; if the tide went out before the scow was emptied the crew could not return to the ship until the next tide many hours later.

So oil drums were rolled onto the beach and boxes of cargo carried ashore in a belt-line performance, men panting out queries and replies about all the happenings of the year since the last visit of the North Star.

With the cargo spread out on shore, there was still some time remaining before the tide would be gone so we had an early morning picnic around an open fire.

So long awaited and so quickly gone, they were soon aboard the launch and headed back for the ship. Bill and I stood on the beach and watched them from sight, thinking of the long spell before we would see these friends again. In reluctant farewell, with dry throats aching we held our eyes on the masts until the relentless shears of distance cut us apart.

Today's North Star visit varies only in the more modern aspect of the new ship. Even the officers and many of the crew are the same as those who manned the wooden icebreaker. The villages are the same lonely spots peopled with friends to whom the brief visit means life-giving supplies as well as a chance for news and conversation.

For us in the Mt. Edgecumbe Community, the North Star is as much a personal friend as to those it serves farther north. Although their homes are in Seattle, the officers and crew are like members of the community. We never heard it whistling down the channel without the shivering thrill that is the peculiar accompaniment to the sight of a dearly loved ship about to embark or return from distant and arduous voyages. Whenever the North Star leaves the channel, the nurses in the BOQ wave bed sheets from the channel-facing windows. (On the afternoon Bob and I returned from the maiden voyage of our 22-foot boat we named Elixir of Sitka, we saw an enormous white sheet fluttering at us from a third-story BOQ window. We never felt more touched and honored.)

Because the Star carries so many passengers to and from their stations and to Seattle to spend leaves outside, it has a few comfortable staterooms. Only ANS personnel and their immediate families are eligible for the small space available, and preference is given to those who are travelling on business. After all patients and official passengers have been accommodated, personnel may use remaining space for nonprofessional traveling. This was the basis on which I might be able to make the trip, and for this reason I would wait until the last moment before knowing whether or not space was available.

What do you pack for such a trip? Answering this question

occupied most of the spring and summer. For at least three months, and possibly much longer, there would be no ducking into a convenient store, not even via shore boat, to buy a toothbrush or a pair of nylons. I especially enjoyed mulling over the poser of what books to take. Many's the night I've put myself to sleep pondering which ten or fifteen books I would take with me to a desert island. Here was a chance to put it to the acid test. I would have more leisure for reading than ever before. Of course, the desert island scenario implies a possible lifetime with the chosen group. Since my acid test would, God willing, let me return eventually to old favorites, the final decision favored unread volumes. The choice turned out a hodgepodge in which I tricked myself by including several heavy tomes on the assumption that days of inactivity would encourage me to read them. Before the journey's end, I had read many times the number of books I took with me and also scoured the ship for reading matter. During the last few weeks, I was saved by a drawer full of dog-eared pocket mysteries Nurse Gaddie kept in her stateroom. And still some of what I brought went unread. I also took my typewriter.

Clothes were a problem, in fact a much knottier problem than I at first foresaw. We would dress for dinner aboard ship; "dressing," meant packing skirts in addition to slacks and outdoor clothing for daytime wear. What I needed most was a heavy waterproof parka. I dispatched Bob on one of his frequent trips stateside to purchase for me a fleece-lined army surplus parka.

It was while he was south on this trip that I became suspicious, in spite of my preoccupation with preparations, of certain unusual physiological symptoms. A trip to the clinic confirmed my suspicions. I was pregnant. This was welcome news, but the timing posed problems. If I had to forego this trip, there would never be another such chance. I did rapid arithmetic. If the North Star kept within its schedule, I would be home with a little less than two months to spare. I am neither a rugged pioneer nor a daredevil. My only trait that may depart from the usual is an overdeveloped curiosity. Sort of like a six-week old kitten, I want to see what's on the other side of the mountain. Curiosity sometimes leads me astray from good sense.

I admit that had I had experience of either the trip to Pt. Barrow or having a baby, I should probably have reluctantly dissuaded myself from going. But I shall always be grateful to that lack of experience and for the good health that gave me the confidence to go ahead. I most certainly do not recommend that all expectant mothers embark on a long and unpredictable sea voyage to remote corners of the earth, but for me, there could have been no better therapy. During a period that at home might have seen me moody and self-pitying, I gave no more than passing thought to discomforts of my condition.

After receiving at least one doctor's approval, (I did not press my luck) only one other consideration gave me pause. I did not wish to cause either embarrassment or concern to the crew and other passengers. I decided that when they saw it was not disturbing to me, they would forget about it. I hope they did. At least I appreciate the fact that not once did anyone confront me with the suggestion that I must have taken leave of my senses, though I've no doubt the idea crossed many minds.

One other deterrent nagged me. For one who loves boats and water so much, I am a rotten sailor. I get seasick. Fortunately, the new drug Dramamine effects almost complete insurance. So I packed a huge supply and used it often. Also at this time, 1950, the relationship between the U.S. and U.S.S.R. was particularly unsteady and unpredictable, and the North Star's route would be very near the International Date Line. Although this gave rise to wild speculations, we all decided the North Star would be as safe as any other part of Alaska.

With all of these hampering thoughts satisfactorily rationalized, the day finally came when at 8 o'clock in the evening I, with my stowaway, stood at the North Star's rail watching the widening strip of water between it and the Mt. Edgecumbe dock. I waved at the receding familiar faces. If there was a moment when I would have reneged on my adventure, it passed quickly.

chapter 4

Across the Gulf to the Aleutians

From Mt. Edgecumbe, the North Star steered directly toward the Gulf of Alaska, on a southerly course, strangely enough. Unimak Pass, the first opening in the Aleutian chain, is far south and west of Sitka. Half an hour after the farewells, we were in rolling outside waters and by morning were out of sight of land. Five days of normal running at the ship's cruising speed of eleven knots or 12.65 mph, ten days were required to cover the distance to our first stop, the twin ports of Dutch Harbor and Unalaska. One knot equals 1 nautical mile which equals 1.15 miles. Use of the term "knot" comes from the early method of measuring a ship's speed by counting the number of carefully spaced knots on a rope let out from a moving vessel and timed with an hour glass calibrated to measure half a minute.

The North Star was loaded so heavily that the heaving gulf merely rocked her gently. At this starting point of the trip, the ship carried not only a capacity load of freight but a full complement of people as well. There were thirty-nine passengers; more than half of them were students and post-treatment patients returning to homes up north. Days of nothing to see except swelling and sinking gray water, overcast sky, and occasionally the adorable parrot-like birds called Puffins gave us sufficient time for orientation to life on shipboard.

Four of the orthopedic boys who had been stellar performers on my radio program were aboard, en route to that mythical- tome home about which they chattered incessantly. They had stars of excitement in their eyes and pockets bulging with odd assortments of the treasures dear to the hearts of small boys. We saw little of them, for the nurse, Mrs. Gaddie, kept them occupied in the sickbay and clinic quarters of the ship.

Remaining passengers were teachers headed for coastal villages. Some of them were returning from summers outside, some being transferred, and some embarking on their first assignments. A youthful couple freshly graduated from a Pennsylvania college were on their way to Unalakleet in Norton Sound. They listened intently and a bit apprehensively to the conversations of experienced teachers. And of course, there were Hazel, Dr. Mary Sherman, and myself who were round-trippers. Also accompanying us was Amos Burg, photographer and world traveler, whose illustrated article on the journey has since appeared in the National Geographic. We were the "tourists."

All of the first night out, I was annoyed by the perpetual creaking in the ship's bulkheads as we swayed from side to side. The scrunching and scratching reminded me of the family of squirrels that once inhabited a corner of the attic directly over my bedroom when I was a child. I reacted with the same frustrated irritation I'd felt toward the squirrels. When I complained about it at breakfast, Mary said she found it a pleasant, soothing sound, reminding her of the creaking of a horse's saddle. I switched associations and soon became friendly with the regular rhythmic noises of the ship.

Daily, Hazel, Mary and I made trips to the bridge to check on navigation. We studied with fascination the pencil line across the chart of the Gulf of Alaska, which showed the forty miles we had made during the previous four-hour watch. Mr. King, the mate who was usually on watch at the hour we chose to pay our wheelhouse visit, was gracious about answering questions and aiding us in keeping accurate track of the ship's route on our maps-our "road maps," as the crew derisively called them.

By the fourth day, we were restless from lack of scenery and lack of exercise. The ship's extensive deck load curtailed the traditional constitutional. After fifteen or twenty paces, the hopeful promenader would meet a stack of lumber forcing a retracing of steps, only to come face to face with a bevy of the ubiquitous oil drums. But on that morning, we awoke to a brilliant blue sky fluffed throughout with white clouds. The Shumagin Islands, beginnings of the Aleutian Chain, were all around us, protecting the water and making it smooth as a mirror. The islands were startlingly beautiful in the sunshine. Since we were already in the part of the world where the timberline is at less than zero altitude, the islands were bare of trees. But they arose sheer out of the sea with a covering of emerald grass on their lower reaches and rose-hued rock above. They looked so much like peaks of the Colorado Rockies in shape and color that it was disconcerting to see them jutting up from blue waters instead of verdant foothills.

Behind us when we arrived on deck was the inverted ice cream cone of Pavlof Volcano, belching out thick, black smoke every three minutes. Belkovski village off the starboard bow was near enough for us to study through binoculars. A clump of low buildings nestled at the foot of one of the green towering peaks monopolized by the disproportionately large white-and-green shape of the Russian Orthodox Church in the exact center of the cluster. Just beyond Belkovski in the next bay was the King Cove Cannery. We encountered a few trollers and seiners, which carried with them a brief breath of home.

The sunshine, the land so near, the sight of other boats, and the serenity of the water combined to convey a sensation of having arrived. It was with considerable shock that I awoke from an afternoon siesta to find us once again pitching through turbulent water.

The morning's deception had emboldened me to forego my prophylactic dose of Dramamine. I gritted my teeth in determination not to display my weakness at this first test and lurched oafishly about the rollicking stateroom trying to dress for dinner. Since all gear had been carefully stowed in deference to the term "shipshape," this meant burrowing under bunks for suitcases. By the time I was "dressed," I could not even have defined equilibrium. Still gripping my pride as a sailor, I stumbled out into the companionway. When minutes later I encountered the Captain and felt the need of some kind of reassuring conversation, I inquired brightly, I thought, "What's rocking the boat?"

Skipper fixed on me a Horatio Hornblower expression and growled, "Hell, there's nothing between us and Australia. That's what's rocking the boat."

In abject humiliation, I turned the proverbial shades of green and dead white and plunged into my stateroom, where I wallowed in misery knowing I could never live through three months of this. By 8 o'clock in the evening, Dramamine and a noticeable flattening of the sea brought me back to life and the society of shipmates.

For the preceding twenty-four hours, the question of whether or not to stop at Akutan to disembark the Akutan teachers had been shuttled back and forth. To their immense relief, the decision had finally been made in favor. They were packed, smiling, and ready. But as we passed the entrance to Akutan Bay at midnight, an angry willawaw, a mini-tornado, whistled across the bow, and we ploughed forward without a backward glance. "Well, it's a typical homecoming greeting," said Mr. Elton philosophically, as he carted suitcases back to their stateroom.

In dismal wind and rain, we tied to the dock at Dutch Harbor, where we would load 800 more drums of oil. There would not be another docking until our return here, months later. From here north, winter ice would systematically wash away any docks built during the summer months. Also, in most cases, the mudflats produced by the great rivers that empty into the Bering Sea prevent any but the most shallow-drafted craft from coming in close to the beaches. Many times, we were unable to anchor even within sight of the village we were visiting.

The dock at Dutch was also the last opportunity to take on water. During the gold rush, all boats headed north stopped at Dutch Harbor for the same reason, and it was here that Robert Service found the inspiration for his epic frontier poem *The Shooting of Dan McGrew.* For three months and possibly more, we must do with only the water carried in the ship's tanks and what small quantity the ship's converters could distill. The tanks do carry enough to keep the boat supplied for three months, with judicious restrictions on showers and laundries. But should conditions delay the schedule, lack of water could become a major hardship. That had happened frequently on the old North Star, we were told.

We were not permitted shore leave. The crews and passengers of previous vessels had on occasion vandalized the vast army and navy warehouses full of valuable equipment left from Dutch Harbor's recent era of military fame and importance. Eight marines and two Standard Oil employees remain to care for this once-gigantic base, and the only reliable protection they can provide is to keep passengers and crew on board ship.

From the deck, we could see an endless layout of glum-looking barracks that once housed 60,000 men. Even when the sky cleared and the sun shone warmly at noon, it was not a heartwarming sight. The desolate aura of a deserted military base was not dispelled. But the topography of the Aleutian mountains with their green velvet carpeting is beautiful to behold.

While Hazel and I sunbathed atop the wheelhouse, Dr. Sherman went ashore and saw four human patients and one canine. The dog, with an old and poorly healing fracture of its right foreleg, was more up her orthopedic alley than the humans, so she brought him aboard for x-ray. This was a prelude to learning the significant position of northern dogs. They are not pets but valued workers, and their welfare is crucial.

We rushed down from sunbathing to use the showers one last time before one of the crew came around to shut them off for the remainder of the trip. And we were underway.

From Dutch, the ship took the forty-five-mile trek back to Akutan to make one more attempt to discharge the Eltons. This time, we found the bay calm. It was eight o'clock, just turning dusk. Fingers of fog drifted between extraordinary pinnacles of rock rising like sentinels out of the glassy sea. Like a painted theater backdrop, the palest of pink streaks lay gently across the horizon of a pearl gray sky. In the foreground, a pod of whales cavorted.

Akutan is a peaceful, whitewashed village of eighty-two Aleuts, snuggled into the foothills about one-half mile from where we dropped the hook. A fleet of five little dories with outboard motors came skittering out to meet us and to carry the Eltons back home with their provisions for the year ahead. From the bridge, we watched spellbound the staging of a fantastic unloading drama.

As darkness fell ship's searchlights spotlighted the ladder down to the dories. They looked alarmingly minute alongside the great hulk of the North Star. Soon the slings were swinging from the booms down to Mr. Elton, who awkwardly maneuvered each of the small boats in turn until it was loaded and sputtered off for shore. The suitcases, crates, and cartons on the sling platform had nothing but the skill of their stacking to prevent them from tumbling into the ocean. We gasped and held our breaths as Mr. Elton shifted one after another of the packages into the dory. We hoped his wife was safely below decks where she could not watch this terrifying procedure and tremble for the welfare of her belongings. She seemed imperturbable, though, and was, of course, standing on deck watching it all with impressive calm.

Within forty-five minutes, all was unloaded, including wife and dog, and we waved farewell to the Eltons as they putt-putted happily away to their village and isolation for another year. Soon we were out of the gulf into the Bering Sea and on our rugged way North. I ruminated; with what apprehension must other couples headed into the coastal wilderness for the first time have witnessed this show and its implications. As it turned out, the unloading of the Eltons was the least hazardous of many such dramas we watched. We came to accept these ordeals as a matter of course so soon that I think we were never again as awed.

Two days later, at 4 o'clock in the afternoon, we entered the mouth of Hooper Bay and lay off a full five miles from shore, behind the shallows created by several small rivers emptying into it. For twenty-four hours, we had rolled through heavy seas and enormous swells. And though our anchorage was protected from the swells, the wind continued to be gusty and the shallow water exceedingly rough. It was so rainy and dim that we could barely make out the outline of the shore, and even through Skipper's powerful binoculars we could not distinguish the village. The ship whistled into the mist and clanged its bell eerily to announce our arrival to the unseen village. Then the Star dropped the hook and we settled back to wait. Before many minutes, Sparks reported from the radio room that a power barge would attempt the trip out and should be sighted within an hour and a half. We adjourned to dinner.

In due time, the outline of the scow was visible careening though the choppy water. We watched with amazement and disbelief as this clumsy craft wallowed toward us, and we wondered how thirty-seven tons of cargo could possibly be transferred from the ship to this unlikely-looking platform in the middle of a convulsive sea.

A power scow, as the name suggests, is a motor-driven barge with no keel. It navigates through heavy sea by sliding sideways up and down the waves. It is a nearly indestructible vessel, but it looks like a harrowing ride for anyone on board. In Hooper Bay, even the scow could not get nearer to the village than one and a half miles. It in turn must discharge the cargo onto smaller boats for final delivery.

The thirty-seven tons we carried for Hooper Bay Village was supplemental to the regular freight delivery, which the Star had made on its previous trip covering the Bristol Bay area, and consisted chiefly in food stuffs, some lumber, gasoline, and metal piping. While the Star with her heavy load and firm anchorage remained quite steady, the little scow bobbed up and down next to us like a cork. Both crews worked feverishly against the hazards of wind, rain, salt spray, and slippery decks. The booms with their winches and carriages rode back and forth from one hold to the other. I had not even imagined the problem of this kind of unloading, much less the method of carrying it out:. watching became compulsive.

Nine days of shipboard restriction went by before we had our first chance to tread on solid earth and to gaze on Eskimo land. For by this time, we were well into the North. This first shore leave came at St. Michael, on the southern lip of Norton Sound, a village of 152 Yupik Eskimos and 2 white men, the port officer and the Roman Catholic priest.

Perfect weather and a clean, well-kept tug made the trip to shore from the ship pleasurable, although our experience was yet too limited for us to appreciate fully the ease with which the jaunt was made.

St. Michael is a village of fabulous historic import. But its landmarks of history have disintegrated to near anonymity. Alaskan pioneers, like all pioneers, have been too intent on solutions and survival to be aware of themselves as creators of history. Unlike the pioneers of the New World, they were not followed quickly enough by others eager to value and preserve the artifacts of their extraordinary lives.

St. Michael was first established in 1833 by the Russians, and of their era, at least one relic remains, a small block house constructed of hand-hewn logs and hand-made copper nails. Its doors swing on enormous beaten copper hinges. But its original roof has been replaced with sheet metal. In 1898, when the Klondikers swarmed into Norton Sound to make their notorious way up the Yukon, St. Michael was a starting point for the sternwheelers. Their skeletons still haunt the tide flats in huge piles of rusted and for the most part unrecognizable scrap iron. When drifters, gamblers, and confidence men became an abhorrently fearsome obstacle to the gold seekers, the U.S. Militia moved in and established Fort St. Michael. For many years thereafter, this was a large, humming community. It was still thriving as late as 1920.

The most spectacular remnant of Fort St. Michael is the sidewalk. St. Michael is the only village in northern Alaska able to boast of such a wonder today. The sidewalk is a web of boardwalks meandering for miles in all directions over the tundra. To be sure, an unwary pedestrian could easily step through one of the countless holes and sustain a fracture, but considering the number and severity of winters these planks have weathered, it is remarkable to see them still winding and walkable through the tall grasses and over the spongy soil. As you stroll this boardwalk far from the little hub of activity near the beach that is today's village, you pass ruins of the rococo false fronts of saloons, restaurants, and department stores with names like The City of Paris. But the traces of grandeur are so faint and so in conflict with the present that it is not easy to summon up a mental reconstruction of the past.

Besides the Roman Catholic Church there stands a former Russian Orthodox Cathedral that must have been nearly as ornate as Sitka's St. Michael's. Now, the closest Orthodox priest is far to the south in the Aleutians. The caretaker has lost the key. Many of the windows are without panes of glass. And such icons and treasures as there are, are piled high with dust.

We were the first ship's passengers to visit the village in five years, and it would be difficult to say who was the more curious about whom. We stared at each other with equal amazement. A more colorful and true-to-legend cortege of Eskimos than those who came out to see and be seen by us would be hard to imagine. Since we were favored by an ideal morning for photography, our cameras were snapping left and right, causing an assortment of reactions from shy embarrassment to twittering giggles.

The only one who spoke more than "Hello" or "Good Morning" was a young teenage girl wearing a tailored suit. She had been a student at White Mountain when Hazel was there. She was delighted to recognize Hazel and chatted lengthily about her hopes to enter the Edgecumbe School after her final year at White Mountain. Absence of conversation from the rest may have been due to shyness as much as unfamiliarity with English, for when questioned directly about names and ages and so forth, they usually responded with understandable, if not necessarily accurate, answers.

Of all the villagers, the favorite was Achukaloa (a phonetic guess at spelling), the medicine man. His English name is Willie Mutt. Achukaloa has a son named Mutt Willie, a nod, I take it, to the Scandinavian custom of giving the son his father's given name as surname. When we clambered off the tugboat Warrior, Willie Mutt was sitting on a tabletop stump, posturing to best show off a pair of knee-high mukluks. With longish hair and chin whiskers framing mongoloid features, he looked like someone I might have expected to meet had I been traveling in Tibet. He was not my preconception of a typical Eskimo or Aleut.

Each time we passed him, Willie Mutt beamed at us and broke into high-pitched giggles. I tried not to be obvious about taking pictures of people, to avoid offending. (I never did get over feeling intrusive about obtruding my camera into people's private lives. I'm sure this reluctance cost me some excellent pictures.) I had resisted the temptation to photograph Willie Mutt several times. Then a wee youngster careening about on a bright red tricycle caught my attention, and I focused my camera for a picture. Willie Mutt just happened to be in the foreground of the shot, and that was ideal for my theme of contrasting the ancient and modern. I thought I could snap it quickly without attracting his attention. But Willie saw the camera immediately, as though he had been watching for just that move. He quickly swung himself into a magnificent pose, prominently displaying grin and mukluks and tittering happily. That may have been just why Willie Mutt was sitting there.

Later, we encountered Willie strolling along the boardwalk. Our "Good Morning" was answered by a neatly pronounced "Good Morning" followed by a long sentence made up of guttural "huck huck hucks" after which he pointed cheerfully to the tops of his gorgeous mukluks and said, "No good!"

St. Michael has one store operated by the Northern Commercial Company. Here, we bought woven baskets and hot-dish pads, some of the chief crafts of the villagers. There were also some items of ivory carving from nearby Stebbins, but the craftsmanship was poor. We were fascinated to see shelves laden with Certo and Krusteaz Pie Crust Mix. We were also interested to see a list of names posted for chest x-rays on the North Star, indicating those slated for new plates and those for rechecks. Some thirty children had been brought out to the ship to see Dr. Sherman during the night, but not one of them was an orthopedic case. We were to discover that this was true most of the time. Plenty of sick people, but no orthopedics. It made no sense, for a stroll through almost every village would reveal one or more outstanding and obvious orthopedic problems. A careful translation of "orthopedic" into terms like "crippled people" or "crooked bones" didn't change things.

Finally, after asking clearly, "have you any crippled children or adults for me to look at?" and receiving a negative reply, Dr. Sherman took to pointing out individuals who could barely hobble down the street and saying, "What about that one?"

"That one? Oh, he's been like that ever since he was born."

So that was the answer. The handicapped adjust. The village accepts. And the malformed of the community are no more considered in need of medical attention than the hardiest hunter.

We sailed north from St. Michael's horizon, with its solid monopoly of volcanic peaks, toward Golovin, directly opposite on the northern lip of Norton Sound.

chapter 5

Night On Fish River

"How would you like to go up the river in that?" the 2nd mate asked me. We were leaning over the rail at about 10:30 at night, watching a flat, open, sampan-type of boat lurch up to the side of the ship. His tone, along with the wildness and darkness of the night and the unlikely appearance of the bomb-boat, as I later learned it was called, reduced my reply to a timorous peep.

"That's exactly what I'm going to do, I guess."

He looked at me in a shocked way, suggesting that he might never see me again, and if I were that great an idiot, it was probably just as well. He backed away, shaking his head, and said nothing more. It was enough to send shivers up and down my spine.

We had reached the entrance to Golovin Bay and dropped the hook there, seven miles out from the village. Golovin is situated at the mouth of the Fish River. And 15 miles up Fish River is White Mountain, where the ANS boarding school for elementary grade Eskimo children is located. By radio, plans had been made

MS North Star at anchor.

Downtown Sitka St. Michael's Cathedral at center.

Mt. Edgecumbe School and Hospital from Sitka Channel.

Alaska
Steamship Co.'s
ALASKA.

Fishing
boats in Sitka's
boat harbor.

PBY seaplane
coming up the
ramp to the turn
around. Most air
traffic to Sitka is
amphibious.

Recess at Baranof Elementary School, Sitka.

The Sitka Madonna. Our Lady of
Kazan painted by Vladimir Borovikovsky.

Gold doors leading to alter room, icons and other
treasures inside St. Michael's.

Gathering on the Mt. Edgecumbe dock to say "Bon Voyage."

Self-conscious Eskimo boys, discharged orthopedic patients, on the deck of the North Star.

Aleutian Village of Akutan.

Power Barge at Hooper Bay.

North Star at Dutch Harbor showing part of the ships extensive deck load.

White Mountain School.

Beach at White Mountain showing bomb boat.

Kotzebue men load sealskin pokes full of seal oil into their boat.

Kotzebue Hospital. Empty oil drums are a ubiquitous part of the Alaska landscape.

The rescued Kobuk in tow.

Skipper admires his birthday presents.
Portrait of his son in scout uniform on bulletin board.

Kotzebue. Winter and summer homes.

Wainright. Passengers ride to shore on barge loaded with sacks of coal.
Ship's launch hurries away to avoid grounding.

Wainright. Sled, dog and sod igloo. Child emerging from the door on the roof.

Sod igloo.

Pt. Lay. Umiak Frame.

Bush pilot landing in lagoon at Pt. Barrow.

Hazel ready to board
plane for flight over the
pole. Pt. Barrow.

Kayak frame and sod igloo.
Wainright.

Whalebone cemetery from a distance. Point Hope.

North Star at anchor viewed from within the whalebone cemetery.

Children at play in Unalakleet.

Boy and his dogs. Pt. Lay.

Dr. Mary Sherman with a Blatchford twin in the ship's lounge.

Mama Blatchford, the twins and Violet.

Bleak Pt. Lay.

Unalakleet. Home, garden, storehouses, and racks of drying fish.

Moe and his crew begin the "tank show." Note man with homemade crutch far right. The great Moe himself at far left.

Elim. Audience gathers in the bleachers to watch Moe and his crew set up oil tanks.

Wainright. Skin boats (umiaks) in tow by tug.

Cape Deceit. Deering.

Kivalina children playing in umiak.

King Island women and children arrive in umiaks to board the North Star.

Eskimo women.

Approaching King Island. Village perches precariously on its perpendicular mountainside.

Ukivok Village, King Island. Schoolhouse at bottom and Catholic Church at top of village.

King Islanders on board the North Star watch the approach to their home.
Picture by Juan Muñoz.

North Star from high atop King Island.

King Island homes built on stilts.

Life returns to King Island.

Winter life on King Island. Ukivok means "place for winter."

Pictures by Juan Muñoz, 1951.

Artwork by Rei Muñoz

Drummer and Dancer

Berry Picker

Cat's Cradle

Fisher Girl

King Islanders greet the North Star.

95

The Stowaway at two years old wearing her fur parky in good Eskimo tradition.

for a boat to come out to the ship from White Mountain to pick up a group of us to visit the school. Besides Hazel, Dr. Sherman, myself, and Carolyn Breidig, another Mt. Edgecumbe nurse, there were Mr. and Mrs. Pettitt, teachers going to Kivalina, and Joe, an Eskimo student from Mt. Edgecumbe who was a former White Mountain student. We had supposed that it would be a daytime trip beginning in the early morning and getting us back in the evening. However, as we drew near to Golovin at 9 P.M., word came over the radio that the boat would be out as soon as it could make it to take us in for an overnight visit. Hence the arrival of this strange looking craft in the middle of the night.

We had Skipper's permission to go. We also had his stern admonition that the ship would not wait for us if we were not back when unloading was finished. And we had his absolute assurance that it was a foolhardy plan. Skipper's warnings were not idle threats. The business of the North Star is to deliver its cargo in the most efficient way. Passengers are tolerated only if they fit their activities to the ship's schedule. If for any reason it is advisable for the ship to move on, and passengers, or even crew members for that matter, are straying ashore, the ship will go, and the wanderers must use their ingenuity to catch up with it at another port of call. Nor is this unreasonable. The North Star costs more than $1,000 a day to operate, and she cannot afford to play mother hen waiting solicitously for her chicks to come home to roost, even for an hour or two. We checked with the freight clerk, Bill Wanzer, who assured us it would take at least 20 hours to unload. Since we planned to be back by early afternoon of the next day, we were satisfied that we had plenty of time

Undaunted by the ominous forewarnings, we, Hazel, Dr. Sherman, and I, donned long underwear, slacks, and parkas and, with camera equipment strapped around us, descended the wobbling ship's ladder into the insecurity of the bomb-boat.

Scrabbling down the Jacob's ladder under the eerie gleam of the searchlight, we must have looked sort of like a pack train of Tibetan Sherpas. Gaddie must have thought so, too. She leaned out of the clinic porthole to take flash pictures of us.

But not all of us wore adequate northern clothing on this side trip. The Pettits had appeared consistently in light summer clothes, complete to Mr. Pettitt's natty straw hat. At first, I thought they were new to Alaska and didn't know any better. But then I learned that they had been teaching for two years in Wales, on the westernmost point of Seward Peninsula, only a few miles south of the Arctic Circle, and with full, experienced knowledge, were transferring to Kivalina as many miles north of the circle. I was baffled. Could there be a shirt sleeves cult in the north? An explanation finally came. They had spent the summer touring southern U.S. states. Their return to Alaska had been fraught with plan changes. They had boarded the North Star unexpectedly and at the last moment, in Seattle. All of their belongings, including heavy clothing, were being transported from Wales to Kivalina while they were away.

The Pettits embarked on our bomb-boat excursion in raincoats; she in a babushka, he in straw hat, and both without boots or rubbers. Joe, the Mt. Edgecumbe boy, was in as bad a fix. He had borrowed a waist-length slicker and except for that had only indoor clothing to protect him from the elements.

When we boarded the bomb-boat, it was already jammed with people. It was altogether too dark even to see what the nearest neighbor looked like, let alone swap introductions. We huddled together anonymously on benches under a tarp that covered perhaps a quarter of the boat. We did recognize Pete, one of the engineers from the ship. His home was in Golovin and he was going in to spend the night. During the seven-mile voyage up the bay those of us from the ship kept up a desultory conversation amongst ourselves. Pete echoed the dubious note on which we had said goodbye to the ship's crew by shaking his head disapprovingly and saying, "I suppose this pilot knows the river well enough to keep off the mudflats." His subtext seemed to suggest that no pilot knew the river that well in the dead of night.

With bravado, we said. "Oh, certainly he does!" But this was the first we'd heard of mudflats.

At the end of an hour, the bomb-boat slid stealthily up onto Golovin beach and discharged three-fourths of the passengers. Then silently, with the nameless shadows that were left, we started into the mouth of the Fish River. By now it was raining hard, and dense fog had settled over all. It was past midnight, and most of the shadows arranged themselves in prone positions on the narrow benches and presumably went to sleep.

We got into the river mouth without mishap, and our pilot began looking for the unlighted oilcan buoys that marked the channel through the shallows. Much zigzagging and searching with a flashlight beam got us past the first few. With a feeling of relief, we would slither around one can. Then immediately an atmosphere of anxious tension would permeate the boat while everyone strained eyes into the murkiness until someone shouted, "There it is!" and the relief-anxiety cycle would begin again. The rain and fog came down more heavily, and the oilcans were spaced so far apart that eventually, it became impossible to spot them, even with the flashlight manned by two crouched strangers in the bow.

There was a hideous grinding screech, a sensation of being sucked downward, and we were stuck on a mudflat. The pilot gunned the motor into screaming reverse. A half-hour of twisting gyrations dislodged us from that mudflat onto another. More gyrations, then a whine, a splutter, and the engine stopped altogether.

During the mudflat maneuvers, no one had thought to man the skiff's painter, which had, naturally, become fouled and chewed to bits in the propeller. The pilot dropped over the stern and disappeared with alarming rapidity into the stygian blackness beyond the boat. He emerged again like some sea creature, dripping and holding the frayed end of the skiff line. This was evidently a sturdy propeller for neither bottom scraping nor the snarled line seemed to have damaged it. The motor was soon roaring reassuringly, and we were off once more.

Another five minutes of buoy searching and again came the sticky suction of the mud and the maddened howl of the motor. An eternity went by in this fashion until at last the pilot exploded in desperation, "I don't know which way to turn!" We were abysmally lost in the mudflats of the Fish River mouth in the pitch black of a cold, wet northern night, many many miles from our halcyon haven, the North Star.

Though we were certainly not in the channel, at the moment we were not stuck. The pilot muttered, "Drop the hook and wait for daylight." And he disappeared again over the side, into the skiff this time, out to hunt for the missing channel.

Being a few weeks before the autumnal equinox, daylight in the land of the midnight sun was fortunately not far off. The three of us, Hazel, Mary and I, had filled our pockets with candy bars as a survival tactic. This much, at least, we had learned about wandering off into the unknown. These we shared with those of the still mysterious shadows who seemed to be alive, and we all sat munching and smoking in the rain, waiting for the return of light and pilot. We did not share philosophical observations on our predicament. In fact there were no spoken words at all. I was impressed by the calm resignation with which one accepts an apparently hopeless situation once in it and seeing no way out. The one indication of stress, although I've never verified the medical probability of this, was that my "stowaway" hiccupped though it all.

Within 45 minutes, the pilot was back and the darkness was lifting. Over my left shoulder, I was startled out of my wits to see what appeared to be a brown and white furry animal huddled on the bench next to me. The creature stirred, and an apparition poked a head full of spikey wet blond hair into my face and said, "What's happening?"

I got a grip on myself and explained what I could of the fantastic series of events we had just been through. None of it seemed to surprise or perturb the creature. She laughed and introduced herself as Miss Talcott, one of the White Mountain teachers. I had an ego-jarring inner glimpse of what I must look like myself. Miss Talcott's wild-animal effect was really a beautiful skin parka with a wolverine ruff.

Daylight let the pilot find the channel. Now we made good headway and, unencumbered by mud, were soon in the river proper. In the early light, we made each other's acquaintance and discovered that one of the night's other dark shapes was the White Mountain School's principal, Mr. Benzell. At 5 o'clock in the morning, we arrived.

Weary, wet, cold, and hungry, we were ushered into the principal's home where Miss Talcott produced memorable coffee, toast, and salmonberry jelly. With every sip of coffee, we came a little more to life. Mr. Pettitt, still wearing a limp reminder of his jaunty straw hat, insisted he could feel the cold seeping out. No one doubted him. Joe, who had been trembling like an aspen leaf for hours, had hurried off at once to the boy's dormitory.

After gulping down three or four slices of toast so ravenously that we scarcely tasted it, we realized that we were eating especially delicious bread and that small Alaska villages have no bakeries. One of the woes of young wives going to the outposts is that they must bake their own bread, an art not often fostered in city-bred young women today. This wonderful bread was baked by the girls in the school. They also manage the cooking and serving of all the meals. There are approximately sixty students at White Mountain, from the elementary grades and up to ninth. The main bill of fare is reindeer meat, which the youngsters prefer to any other. This is a source of some discontent among the teachers and other employees who eat in the main dining hall. But at least it is readily available and nourishing.

White Mountain, as Hazel assured us, is undoubtedly situated in quite lovely surroundings, particularly in the winter, when the river and all of Golovin Bay are frozen over, and in the spring, when the ice breaks up. Its residents repeatedly told us what a great summer they'd had, what wonderful hunting and fishing they'd enjoyed. But our point of view was somewhat jaundiced, even after sleeping from 6 to 10 o'clock. Unpleasant rain continued to pour down, and the gumbo mud we wallowed through to get from place to place did not inspire our admiration.

Our stay was short and spent almost entirely sleeping; up at 10:00 for breakfast and off again in the bomb-boat at 11:00. On the previous trip, all the boy students had been deposited in Golovin to find longshore work unloading the North Star and to spend the night in an ANS-owned storehouse on the beach. This trip was to be the girls' outing, and the boat was loaded with the makings of a picnic. These comprised several cartons of dried fish, a huge kettle of fresh water for coffee, and a dozen or more excited, squealing Eskimo girls who stacked themselves in tiers in the bow of the bomb-boat.

This time, enough tarps were provided to protect all of the boat except the pilot's position in the stern. But although the weather grew increasingly squally, to remain under the tarp was to court suffocation and disaster from the odor of dried fish and too many people, not a few of whom were seasick. Hazel, Mary, and I held enough of it open to keep our heads out and suffered instead the risk of drowning from a persistent downpour and the heavy salt spray that broke over the bow and crashed along the length of the boat with every plunge into the choppy water. The trip down river was so uncomfortable and rough that even the exuberance of the schoolgirls was squelched. Most of them were in fright for their lives.

If the river was stirred up, the bay was turbulent. Both the pilot and a helper he had brought insisted that the bomb-boat could not make the trip from Golovin out to the North Star. We accepted their edict without argument. But this posed the problem of finding other transportation. We felt reasonably sure that we were still hours early, relying on Bill Wanzer's estimate. But Skipper's warnings rang in our ears, and we were uneasy. As we drew near the beach, we saw an empty barge and tug standing idle off shore, an ill omen that nearly panicked us.

On shore, we were greeted by the boys from the school, with the news that a barge just looming on the horizon was the first to come in since the ship anchored. Since the empty barge was not working, that meant the loading had been finished on one barge. Must we find a plane to take us to Kotzebue?

Then we were joined on the beach by a covey of drenched and harassed strangers who had just arrived on a plane from Nome. They included a man from the lightering company responsible for the cargo and barges, who was blustering and irate with the Star for having arrived ahead of schedule, and a handful of new passengers; a representative of Alaska Native Industries from Seattle, two nurses from Bethel, and two social workers, one from Nome and one from Mt. Edgecumbe. A more bedraggled and anxious segment of humanity than the lot of us would be hard to find. But our spirits perked up with the arrival of these people, as did theirs at sight of us. The more of us there were, the greater the odds of us getting back to the ship. When Pete the engineer, joined the group, we felt still more hopeful.

Our luck held. The tugboat skipper said he was making another trip out to the ship with us and back in with the disembarking passengers. We leaped eagerly aboard, scarcely saying polite farewells to our hosts, and were off on a fittingly harrowing ride through a short, choppy sea. The storm riling Norton Sound produced the kind of unpredictable and treacherous breakers that trouble seamen in Lake Michigan's most violent storms. Our tug was just the wrong length to manipulate the turmoil easily, and we took green water over the wheelhouse all the way.

Remembering how we had shuddered at the bobbing of the power scow in Hooper Bay, we speculated on how we must look to those on the ship as we hove into sight and then disappeared into every wave. They were all lining the rail to watch us, cameras pointed. Much maneuvering and many failures happened before we were finally secured to the ship, and no attempt was made to lower the ladder. Instead, the freight sling swung down and we were lifted aboard, four at a time. Surely better than a fifty-cent ride in any amusement park.

The sling ride was fun. We loved it, a much easier way to get up and down the steep side of the ship than climbing the swinging ladder. But for some of the others, it was a terrifying moment. The little fellows from the Orthopedic Hospital were among those leaving, and more heart-melting expressions than the terror frozen on their small faces I hope I never see. A couple with two small children were just as frightened. As we guessed, the tug had looked to them as though it might swamp at any moment. They thought they would never survive to see Teller Mission, their destination. The sling trip at least was over quickly, and once they were in it, perhaps the tugboat seemed less hazardous. Back aboard, we were greeted with the anticipated "I told-you-so's" by Skipper and Sig, the chief steward, and were berated for holding up the ship. But we were so exhausted that they took pity on us and postponed their teasing. We had supper, an unusually silent one, and went directly to bed, with no intention of rising for breakfast.

However, at 8 o'clock in the morning, Tommy, our jovial

waiter, pounded on my door and called that he was saving a place at table. Too befuddled to demur, I dressed in seconds and reeled groggily out to the dining hall. I was grateful to Tommy, for that morning we passed Cape Prince of Wales and could see the Diomede Islands. The coast of Siberia appeared on the radar but wasn't visible through the mist.

Most of the day, we three spent concocting an elaborate medal for Skipper out of an unfolded sputum cup lining. It was an enormous, garish medallion festooned with all the scraps of brilliant colors we could find amidst our gear. It was bestowed "For Heroism and Patient Forbearance Above and Beyond the Call of Duty." We hoped it would mollify him.

CHAPTER 6

Kotzebue, Crossroads of the North

On the 22nd of August, we crossed the Arctic Circle to the accompaniment of enough horseplay to do justice to any equator crossing. The nonsense began at breakfast and moved along at an accelerated pace until the evening climax with the visit from King Neptune and his court. Sig hovered about all day wearing a smug, elfish twinkle and delivering himself of ominous warnings about what might happen when King Neptune rose from the deep and came over the bow to call all first-timers to atone for their trespasses. Skipper wore the impassive face of a sphinx.

The twelve-hour preparation was part and parcel of the activities. We could not resist making matters worse by responding with jibes about what we might do to Father Neptune. We speculated loudly on how surprised he might be to find himself ceremoniously ushered back into the ocean after he had held his court.

We were promised a feast of ice worms and muktuk, a whale skin and blubber delicacy prized by Eskimos. During lunch, a tin can was passed to a jubilant Sig, who examined it superciliously and in full view before stowing it in the refrigerator. After lunch, the crew held a private strategy meeting in the social hall. Since they were all in attendance, we could have absconded with the can and possibly thrown a small wrench into the plans. But we thought of it too late. At dinner, we made an abortive attempt to lure the dishwashers out of the galley to have their pictures taken. Hazel was to slip in and raid the icebox unnoticed. But they were either wise to us or genuinely camera shy, and it didn't work.

At 9 o'clock, the fire alarm sounded. The abandon-ship alarm sounded. The bell clanged. The whistle bellowed crazily. And the ship ground to a halt and dropped anchor on the Arctic Circle. Passengers and crew who were going north for the first time or lacked papers to prove otherwise were herded into the dining hall. Weird gnome-like creatures faintly resembling familiar crewmembers gamboled about, armed with gigantic whalebone paddles, and they countenanced no unnecessary chatter or back talk.

All day, a whispering campaign had been underway to the effect that King Neptune would certainly give those "women tourists the works." We decided to give no one the satisfaction of seeing that we were intimidated and stayed in our dressed-for-dinner skirts instead of donning more comfortable slacks.

Moe, the 1st Mate, as Neptune's police chief, accompanied by members of his force, came down to capture victims one at a time. Under the stimulus of flourished paddles, each blindfolded first-timer was escorted upstairs to the court. Sitting and waiting was painful. Hazel's turn came, then mine. I stood blindfolded amid a babble of voices, feeling foolish, not knowing exactly where I was or who was watching.

My sins were intoned to the potentate:

(1) Making nasty remarks about His Majesty. (Never suspecting that Skipper himself would be Neptune we'd had played our quips and threats in the wrong quarters.)

(2) Arriving late for "King's Navigation School." (Mr. King, mate on the 8-to-12 watch, when we made our trips to the bridge to check on location and other problems of navigation, got this razzing from the rest of the crew for putting up with us.)

(3) And my most heinous crime, husband desertion.

Sentence was pronounced in bellowing tones by the monarch: twelve blips with a paddle for these transgressions. Then, with shoes and stockings removed, I was coerced into stepping into the Bering Sea, a tub of tepid water, and from there into the Arctic Ocean, a tub of chilled water and floating ice cubes.

After the immersion came a haircut, the hallmark of a "Shellback." I was comfortably sure they would not shave a stripe through my hair. But the simultaneous whirring of an electric razor and sprinkling on of shredded rope were alarmingly realistic. When the ritual was finished and I put up an investigating hand, the bits of frayed hemp felt distinctly like newly clipped hair.

The repast followed. As prophesied, the "hairy ice worms" were easily recognized cold spaghetti, but the "muktuk" was dreadful chunks of salt pork, on which everyone gagged. The meal concluded, I was pronounced "Sister Shellback," the blindfold removed, and the next victim called up.

It was hilarious to watch for a while. But after the passengers, there were a goodly number of crewmembers to be initiated, and the hazing became more vigorous. The social hall overheated. And the school children crowding around and breathing down the backs of our necks kept up a noisy accompaniment with their staccato gum chewing. Say what you will about the white man's firewater; but, whoever introduced bubble gum to the unspoiled children of the North ought to be shot at sunrise.

The visit from King Neptune was a shock to the passengers who had come on board the evening before at Golovin. They were not yet oriented to life on shipboard and unprepared for such uproar and hi jinx. They did not have the benefit of our special buildup, and although this saved them from falling into the trap we did of personally arousing "Neptune's" ire, they were dragged from their rooms and propelled into the madness without having the least idea what was happening.

We wound up the evening listening to Skipper and Sig recount anecdotes of equator crossings. The best of these occurred on one of Byrd's Antarctic expeditions. Moe was with Skipper on this voyage, and it was his first crossing. Skipper was to be Davy Jones and was armed with a long-sheathed saber. In the afternoon, when he happened to have the saber with him, Skipper saw what he mistook for Moe coming down a ladder from the wheelhouse. He planted the most terrific wallop he could muster on the descending bottom. There was a verbal explosion, and the apoplectic face of the Admiral himself peered down, roaring "Wot hoppened?" A weak-kneed and horrified Skipper streaked pell-mell for his cabin. And poor innocent Moe got the beating of his life in the festivities that night.

Long after midnight, we drooped to bed and the ship got underway once more.

The next morning, I arrived sleepily on deck several minutes after 7:30 to find that we were in Kotzebue. That is, we were anchored twenty miles out in Kotzebue Sound, as near as we could get to the shore. The first tug and barge had arrived. The barge was loaded and would leave for Kotzebue at 8 o'clock for those who wanted to go. We moved speedily, if not efficiently.

Since the trip to shore would take six or seven hours, we wrapped up breakfast rolls to take along. We expected to stay overnight. I carried only what I could get into my camera gadget bag: toothbrush, lipstick, comb, washcloth, pen, wallet, and the standard emergency candy bars. This limited my gear to what could be slung around my neck and shoulders.

All the passengers and the freight clerk, Bill Wanzer went. Wanzer's job was to check the cargo as it was put ashore. Last year the freight had been checked only as it left the ship. A large amount of freight destined for inland locations had gone missing never reaching its destination. Since it hadn't been checked by an ANS crew ashore, it wasn't possible to make legal accusations, although there seemed little doubt where the responsibility lay. So Bill Wanzer was stuck ashore for the duration. And a long duration it turned out to be. The North Star's crew had exhibited a notable lack of interest in visiting Kotzebue, even Gaddie, who usually went ashore at every stop was pleased to stay comfortably on board ship.

We rode on the freight-loaded barge, which conveniently carried both the ambulance and the pick-up truck. As many as could found seats in the vehicles. The rest deposited themselves about on the freight. The three of us claimed the back of the pick-up and before long arranged a tarp so we could stretch out in the truck and attempt to catch up on the sleep we'd missed thanks to the visit from Father Neptune. We looked comfy, as onlookers remarked enviously, but it was no substitute for an inner spring mattress. Besides, a steady stream of people posted themselves all over the truck to take pictures of us from various angles.

The trip took seven and a half hours, aided and abetted by the pettishness of the engine in the decrepit tug that towed us. We reached the beach having seen no evidence of another tug coming out and were met by more people taking more pictures. We manipulated our stiff joints out of the truck, off the barge, and into the gloom of what proved to be main street, Kotzebue.

The day was hot and sultry and the stench was overpowering, compounded by filth, dogs, drying fish, seal oil, and an indefinable rank odor that simply rose out of the ground. One Archie Ferguson, about whom we had already heard, supplied the lightering service and, as was soon evident, monopolized most of the town. We knew that Archie would be in constant radio contact with the ship, so our first aim was to locate him and arrange to keep track of the pace of the unloading to avoid being left behind. This was not difficult to do. Archie was as busy as a gopher and very much in evidence. He was hopping back and forth between the barges and the warehouse, his mouth going noisily a mile a minute, emitting streams of malapropisms and vulgarities. Archie was a rotund five by five, whose unpleasantly frenetic appearance had a distinctly lascivious cast.

Our next goals were to find something to stave off the starvation that was rapidly setting in and to locate beds for the night. We followed the crowd to Archie's restaurant, the Kotzebue Grille, "The World's Farthest North Restaurant," where we waited hours for some unsavory sandwiches and coffee. Thus sustained we parted ways, Hazel and Dr. Sherman heading for the hospital and I staying to scout local housing in case the hospital could not accommodate us.

At this point we encountered what we considered an infuriating and unacceptable breach of courtesy that can only be attributed to the sometimes arrogant self-indulgence of doctors. I, of all people, certainly don't begrudge doctors their all too few recreation breaks, but this one was not just thoughtless it was insulting. Dr. Sherman had been looking forward to the fact that, Dr. Rabeau, the ANS doctor in charge of the Kotzebue Hospital, would be back from a medical meeting in

Mt. McKinley and in residence during our visit. Dr. Rabeau would be able to line up patients for her so that her visit would serve a more useful and informative purpose. Not only that; but, Dr. Philip Moore, Chief of Orthopedics at Mt. Edgecumbe, who promoted this trip for her, had come back to Kotzebue with Dr. Rabeau. Mary had anticipated a productive visit. What Hazel and Mary Sherman found when they reached the hospital was that not only had Rabeau and Moore gone blithely off sheep hunting. They had not even informed the nurses at the hospital that we were on board the North Star. Nor had they left us so much as a greeting. Foolishly I had hoped for mail. Worse yet not only had everyone, including both doctors, known for hours about the North Star's arrival, but we had actually reached the beach an hour before they left. Hazel's and my outrage was merely at the absence of common politeness. But Mary's was a matter of official business and we were incensed on her behalf.

We swallowed our hurt pride and, after a few unprintable remarks and epithets, deciding to forget the medical profession we ambled down the main street to what passed for a hotel, the most likely place to find a night's lodging. Unfortunately we'd delayed too long. The other North Star passengers had gotten there first, and the rooms were all taken save one small one at the back with four cots arranged around the walls so that heads and feet met and almost overlapped. Calico curtains hung over the doorway substituting for a missing door. The Hansons, who owned the building, had moved in so recently that they had not yet completed their plans for the hotel, whatever they may have been.

Along with the less than satisfactory door-less room, we found no electricity and no running water. Since this was our first encounter with the water dilemma of the Arctic, it is perhaps pardonable that we were a trifle put off. The ubiquitous chemical toilets would be high on my list of reasons for not living in the frozen North. As to the electricity, Archie owned all of the dynamos in Kotzebue, and since he was at the moment wroth with the Hansons, he had shut theirs off. They had a generator of their own on order, but so far it hadn't arrived.

After establishing ourselves in the "hotel" we ventured forth to view and photograph the metropolis of Kotzebue. And there was plenty to view. With the advent of the air age, the natives of Kotzebue discovered the potential of gaining livelihood from tourists. They are professionally picturesque. There's no denying the authenticity of the place, but it is curiously marred by a prevailing attitude of the Eskimos showing their wares - in this case, the way they live and work. They seem to expect to be photographed. The meandering tourist is greeted with cheery but slightly obsequious "good mornings" and "good afternoons." It's hard to put a finger on, but there is a missing innocence.

Kotzebue's main street is a narrow, muddy rut lined with stores, a movie house called the Midnight Sun Theater, and thronging with parky and mukluk clad pedestrians. The traffic is fearful. I know this sounds absurd, since Kotzebue has just six vehicles, two of which came in with us from the North Star; two pickup trucks, an ambulance, a fire truck (not used for it's original purpose), a tractor, and a large truck that operates as an airport limousine. These six monsters careen madly up and down the one narrow, well-populated street, apparently driven exclusively by operators under twelve years old. They scatter men, women, and dogs helter-skelter. I think I'd as soon dodge the traffic of Chicago.

Dogs are everywhere in the Northland. In the winter, they are the only reliable lifeline, and their well-being is placed only slightly lower than that of people. But in summer, they are a nuisance. They are chained to stakes all over the village, not well fed or cared for. Their thick winter coats shed to a raggedy unkemptness, and they are lean, wild creatures made dangerous by their restraint. One estimates the length of their tether and keeps well out of reach. All night long in Kotzebue, they fill the air with wolfish howls and add an ominous, mysterious note to the breathless summer darkness. Of course, there are puppies galore and the puppies are adorable. They bumble about at will, practicing their growls on anyone who will pay attention. A malamute pup is as appealing as a bear cub.

The Eskimos live through the winter in log and sod hovels and in the summer move into skin tents often jury-rigged next door to the hovels. This combination of winter home and summer home, with the inevitable rack of drying fish in front, is an irresistible camera subject. Nowhere are the contrasts between the primitive and the conventionally modern more in evidence than in Kotzebue. Eskimos here have had a fair amount of exposure to white people. There are eighty or more Caucasians in Kotzebue besides the sizeable number of tourists who come here to catch a glimpse of the far North. The Eskimos have latched onto many modern ways and products, and at the same time, they cling to their native culture. The result is manifest in such curious spectacles as Venetian blinds at the windows of a sod igloo, a rayon jersey dress with tiers of flounces billowing beneath a fur-trimmed calico parky and above a pair of sealskin mukluks, or the powerful outboard motors that propel their umiaks. An old Eskimo man galumphing down the path may be smoking his cigarette in a gleaming aluminum Kirsten holder.

On our way along the street, we stopped at Wiens Alaska Airlines to check on a flight for Caroline Breidig, who was leaving the Star to fly to Nome. Wiens combined its airline office with a Roadhouse proprieted by two snappy, vivacious young women. In Alaska, roadhouse has a meaning entirely apart from the connotations it has elsewhere. In this case, it is literally a house by the side of the road where travelers may find food and

114

possibly lodging between flights. A comforting accommodation this can be, too, in a place where it's common to be stranded by weather for an indefinite length of time.

This looked to us like a huge improvement over Archie's Grille, and we stayed for dinner. The Roadhouse managers were both licensed pilots and had allied themselves with the airline hoping to do some bush flying. So far, they had been unable to get access to a plane and were serving meals to tourists, a breed they mostly found irksome. During the summer just past, there had been 2,000 tourists through the town. Most of them had been sold a trip across the Arctic Circle and were bemused and not very pleased by Kotzebue. In that respect, we joined their ranks. The more we observed of the place, the less desirable it seemed to be.

With the hot and satisfying meal warming our insides and mellowing us into more agreeable humans than we had been all day, we hiked up to the hospital, where the head nurse, Miss Connally, offered us hot water for baths and shampoos. There is no more hospitable gesture anyone in this part of the world can make to a wayfarer. A bath is like a box of Kleenex or a pound of coffee was in the days of wartime rationing.

The Kotzebue Hospital has running water by virtue of a well they have had dug at great effort and expense, although it is still the same sour, unpotable stuff as elsewhere. For drinking, they must use purified rainwater. To heat water enough for so many baths, it was necessary to heat up the entire living quarters of the hospital to a most uncomfortable degree for such a sultry summer night. As I say, it was an act of utmost charity.

Cleaned, nourished, rested, and sipping a cooling drink with ice cubes! in it, life began to look better to us. We spent the evening chatting and drying our hair and deciding that the hospital staff had done the best job of creating a pleasant existence of anyone in Kotzebue.

We walked back to Hanson's in the close, black night, with the dogs moaning and howling around us and shadowy parkaed forms emerging and vanishing into the dark. At the Arctic Adventurers Club, a dance was in progress, but we were not tempted. Back at our temporary dwelling, we stumbled about in absolute darkness until we found our cots and slept fitfully through the stuffy night, resolving to take the first available transportation back to the civilized North Star. Thus ended the first of many days in Kotzebue.

When we had first come ashore, we had learned that the seedy vessel that brought us in was the only one presently able to run at all. There were others being tinkered with but not yet operable. A larger and more powerful tug, the Kobuk, was coming down from Point Hope. When it arrived, it would make trips every four hours to and from the ship, which would make our return a piece of cake, comparatively speaking. A day and a half of sightseeing was plenty to satisfy our curiosity about Kotzebue. We would take a few more pictures in the morning and then go down to see the Diomeders, a family from Little Diomede Island 123 miles away, who came over for the summer in their skin boats to sell ivory carving. And then we would go back to the ship. What optimists we were!

At 7 o'clock in the morning, we were up and dressed and out to seek breakfast. This kind of thing apparently is not done in Kotzebue. The Grille was shuttered, and no signs of life were abroad. We stood in the empty street pondering the next move when Archie came rolling toward us. We asked him what time the restaurant would open.

He glowered at us and snapped, "You're up early for tourists." Rudely he informed us that "everyone had been up until 4 A.M. and probably it wouldn't open until noon. Maybe it wouldn't open all day." Twenty-four hours in Kotzebue already had us wondering how Archie had managed to stay alive so long.

We were still smoldering from Archie's rebuff when a man came out from the rear of the Grille and gawked at us in surprise. We inquired of him if there was anywhere one might obtain a cup of coffee. He said there was no one in the restaurant, but there was a pot of coffee and why didn't we go in the back door and help ourselves. We did. On the way, we met a young Eskimo woman who claimed she did not work there but indicated the bread, butter, and toaster to us anyway. We made toast and ferreted some jam out of a refrigerator, essential to counteract the taste of the rancid butter. We had just finished draining the pot to the grounds when Archie bounced in. He was nonplussed to see us there and clearly disgruntled at finding the coffeepot empty. We neither sympathized nor felt guilty.

We left the price of breakfast on the counter and went out to locate Bill Wanzer to find out about getting back to the ship. It seemed that the Kobuk had lost its propeller en route and was now helplessly adrift somewhere between Kotzebue and Point Hope and awaiting rescue. One tug was still out with the North Star, and two more were not yet in commission. Bill suggested that we might get the Diomeders to take us out in their skin boat. It was speedy and ought to get us there in 45 minutes. A skin-boat ride was intriguing and anything that would get us there in so short a time sounded like a gift from heaven. We concluded an agreement with the Diomeders to take as many as wished to go for $1.00 a person and to leave from the barge that served as a loading dock at 3 o'clock in the afternoon.

The skin boat, or umiak, is a marvelous Eskimo invention. Umiak roughly translated means "women's boat" and is so named because among Greenland Eskimos, the men are said to have a prejudice against using oars, so only women do the rowing. In Alaska there is no such prejudice, and in any case, today a self-respecting owner outfits his umiak with one or more outboard motors. The Diomeders used two big Evinrude motors.

Eskimos learned centuries ago that spruce makes an ideal wood for the skeletal frames of the umiaks, recognizing the same qualities of strength and lightness that also make it suitable for airplane frames, and driftwood spruce abounded on their beaches. Umiaks are flat-bottomed, dory-shaped boats of bearded seal or walrus skin stretched taut over the wooden frames. They are generally from 30 to 35 feet long, and the six or seven cleaned and scrapped hides required to cover them are stitched together by the women with braided caribou sinew. Eskimo women are able to make a seam which, when soaked and swollen, is completely waterproof. It is, in fact the only truly waterproof seam known to be made by any people, European or other. If an Eskimo woman sees anyone rubbing grease into a boot seam she has sewn she feels it as an insult. It implies distrust of her sewing. In the case of the umiaks, however, it's customary to rub grease on the seams just before launching when the boats are dry. Once water soaked they never leak.

When the white whalers first came to the north coast of Alaska they viewed the beach driftwood with contempt and brought with them lumber, which they assured the Eskimos, would be much better for their umiaks. The Eskimos were talked into this. But it didn't take long for them to find that a frame made of spruce was both lighter and stronger than one made of commercial lumber. It wasn't until World War II and its demand for spruce as framework for airplanes that the white men realized the Eskimos had been right all along.

An umiak's light weight and flat bottom give it a negligible draft, even when loaded to capacity. It is ideal for shallow water and for beaching and can be carried easily by three or four men, or even by two one at each end if they are stout enough. It is a hard boat to damage because of its pliancy. Even if one of the wood struts breaks, in an unexpected encounter with a sharp rock say, nothing more serious than a dent in the side of the boat results. Since Eskimo women are not given to the vanity of spike heels, there is little danger of puncturing the stout skins, but if a rip does occur, the same homemade process that originally produced the boat easily patches it.

The bearded seals that furnish skins for the covers weigh from six to eight hundred pounds. They will have been killed during the winter or the previous summer. A month or two before it is time to make the skin boats the hides are put into tubs or bags and kept in a warm place until the hair rots off. When the hair is scraped off one side and the fat off the other side, the skins are ready for sewing and shaping.

A kayak is in some ways an even better boat that the umiak. It has the outline of a racing shell. The frame is made of light wood and whalebone and the entire craft is closed in so that the waves can dash over it without entering. The Eskimos would wear waterproof skin "shirts" that fastened tight around the neck and wrists and around the mouth of the kayak in such a way that even if the boat capsized no water could get into it. A skilled boatman could right himself even in fairly heavy weather. This allows them to go places no other boat would chance. A special use for the kayak is spearing caribou when they are swimming in lakes or rivers.

A skin boat, with its translucent bottom and sides, looks as frail as a breath of summer air. It's hard to believe that one could float safely on a pond, much less make a lengthy ocean voyage carrying twenty or thirty people and their gear. But a large umiak can carry more than twenty drums of oil or as many as fifty people with a draft of only ten inches.

During the morning, as we revisited the hospital and the roadhouse, we discovered that an umiak ride was a novelty even to the permanent residents of Kotzebue. Sensing a way to partially return the kindnesses they'd shown us, we invited Miss

Connally and the girls from Wiens to make the trip out to the ship with us. They leaped at the opportunity.

We gathered together our sparse gear, made the main street rounds to say "goodbye," and went down to the waterfront to board the skin boat. There were, I think, sixteen of us: most of the ship's passengers, our guests, and five or six Diomeders. The Diomeders were poised, intelligent-looking boys, tall for Eskimos. A sizeable crowd gathered once more to watch us embark.

Riding in an umiak is a thrilling experience. It skims over the water with more assurance than most small boats. I speak with some authority, for on this trip, I ventured onto the ocean in more varieties of small craft than most people even see in a lifetime. By reputation, the umiaks' buoyancy makes them well-nigh impossible to swamp and able to withstand almost any weather. I am inclined to believe this, although I'd draw a line somewhere. The weather we encountered on this jaunt is just about where I would draw that line.

The smothering heat suddenly vanished. A wind came up, and a mist closed in. The Diomeders did not know where the North Star was anchored. They had counted on being able to see the ship as soon as they were a few miles out from land. But we never had a glimpse of it. They worriedly scrutinized a big box compass they hand carried. They seemed not to know which direction to head. We bounded hither and thither over the waves. The weather got worse and worse. Eventually they admitted that they could not find the ship and were fearful of running out of gas. They asked if they could go back. We said, "Of course." "Don't question the man at the helm" was a motto we had adopted early. In another hour, we were back on the beach of Kotzebue, which the Diomeders were able to find like homing pigeons, and Archie was razzing us nastily.

The ship had been radioed that we were on our way out in a

skin boat and that we had not made it. Sig sent a message that he had prepared steaks for a welcome-back dinner, which had been "tossed overboard" when we failed to show. This was the first of many such "encouraging" messages from Sig.

The nurses invited us to come have potluck with them and stay the night at the hospital. The Diomeders, who were conscientious young men, felt badly about the fiasco and would have refused payment. But since they had used their gas, and a ride in a skin boat was well worth a dollar, we insisted on paying them. They offered to try again in the morning, weather permitting, and suggested 6 o'clock as a likely hour. We promised to be on hand.

Food was seriously short in Kotzebue at this time. There had not been a freighter all summer. The expected one had burned to the water line. They had not yet been able to lay in their winter rations. So giving us dinner was another Good Samaritan deed. We scrambled eggs and had cold ham and fruit salad. There were two very rotten eggs out of a dozen marked "airborne" and priced at $1.50 (a dozen eggs in Seattle were $ .35).

That night, the weather became much worse, and although it had settled down somewhat by morning, it was still unpromising. None the less, we were up at 4:45 as scheduled. From the hospital dining room, we could see the water where the Diomeders would have to pass in their umiak to get to the dock. So we stayed at the breakfast table and watched. There was no lift in the wind and fog. Some of the Kotzebue aroma was dispelled by the wind. Or maybe by now we were inured to it.

After a while, we grew restless and hiked down to the waterfront to see if there was any activity that might produce a ride. A tug was supposed to have left the ship at 9 o'clock the night before, but there was still no sign of it. Another tug had started out at 3 AM from shore. All the passengers who had elected not to chance the Diomeders again had gone on that tug. But after three hours of drenching and buffeting, they had given up and returned. Everything was at a standstill.

We then ambled up past the hospital to where the Diomeders were camped. Their camping technique was to beach the umiak and set up housekeeping in it. This morning, the boat was upside down on the beach, presumably with the whole family asleep under it. We decided against knocking and returned to the hospital.

By 8:30, other people were stirring, and the regular hospital breakfast was being served. Mr. Dykes, from Deering, came in for breakfast, and the conversation switched from our predicament to talk of archeological research in progress along the north coast. A Danish archeologist, Dr. Helge Larsen, was presently unearthing findings in caves inland from Deering that indicated buried villages going back as far as a thousand years. These and the findings in the ancient village of Ipuitak at Point Hope give evidence of little or no change in the Eskimo cultural patterns from that time to this.

Mr. Dykes eventually made a tremendous hit with us when he said he was sure he could persuade someone named Louie to take us back to the ship in his cabin cruiser. Our faith in the Archie Ferguson flotilla was worn thin. Mr. D. would go at once to find Louie and arrange it. Since Louie worked for him and he was willing to give him the afternoon off, we thought our problem solved. Very soon he was back with the news that Louie's boat was out searching for the lost Kobuk. As soon as it came in, Louie would be delighted to take us. Another bubble burst.

Mr. Wilson, the ANS administrator for the area north of Deering, joined us for coffee. He was scheduled to board the North Star for the trip to Barrow. But he had lived in northern Alaska long enough to be imbued with the pervasive philosophy of relax and wait, where transportation is concerned. Moreover, he was comfortably situated at home while he waited. His wife had entertained us graciously with cookies and coffee served in bone china cups. Although it had seemed distinctly out of keeping with our filthy jeans and disheveled appearance it had been an entirely refreshing and pleasant experience. Mrs. Wilson had the refined appearance of someone you would never expect to be content in an outpost like Kotzebue. Yet she told us that while she was back in the states this year she was nearly frantic until she could secure passage for a return to Alaska.

Mr. Wilson also had a reservation for a plane to Wainwright in case he missed the Star. So his calmness did not relieve our anxiety. In fact, he added to our worries with news that the tug and barge that had left the ship the night before had gone missing, that another tug had gone to look for them and was now lost, and the third and only remaining tug had gone to search for the other two. Counting the Kobuk, this made four missing tugs, five if you counted Louie's cabin cruiser. It was no longer a mystery to us why the crew did not care to come ashore at Kotzebue.

Tuning into the North Star's ship-to-shore conversations on the hospital radio, we were still getting Sig's messages: "Tell those 'tourists' there's no place like home. Maybe this will teach them not to go wandering." We were, of course, desperately anxious to get back just to clean up and rest. By now, the happy effects of the hospital bath were in the far past. Our jeans, sox, and underwear were stiff to the cracking point. But beyond that, we were genuinely afraid Skipper would become disgusted with the Kotzebue dance of inefficiency and weigh anchor for Wainwright. The Kotzebuites were worrying about the same thing, not because of us but because of their freight.

Another stroll down to see Bill W. netted us nothing except that he would send word to the hospital whenever anything was ready to go. Poor Bill looked haggard.

We had become such an accustomed sight on the street that we were greeted familiarly by everyone we met and often invited in for coffee. We began to learn the ins and outs of Kotzebue society. We met many gracious and generous people whose kindnesses we could never repay. We also found a plethora of escapists, which, I suppose is not surprising. There was a sort of "to hell and be damned" survival attitude. And we began to be privy to local gossip. Such as the fact that Archie had a native wife who lived somewhere up river and refused to either divorce or associate with him. His mistress, Beulah, ran the Grille and put up with the rest of his peccadilloes including his "sleeping around" and cheating as inefficiently as he ran his other businesses. How he obtained such control over a community is a mystery. We were informed though, that the chief pastime of the City Fathers was "sleeping with the natives." There was plenty of indignant chattering about this fact but no one seemed unduly perturbed. Just another element of the far North.

Residents of Kotzebue at that time anticipated momentary invasion by the Russians. They had been warned that invasion was likely to occur during the winter and were uneasy about the months ahead. There was an exaggerated notion of a network of communists. They seemed to feel that they had been seriously infiltrated, though I never heard who or where the infiltrators were. One resident told me that she planned to become wealthy when the Russians arrived, by organizing the local native girls and charging for the sexual favors she knew they'd bestow anyway.

Often they would query me about communism in Sitka, which surprised me so completely that I had no answer. It seemed to me that if the Russians were foolish enough to invade the north coast of Alaska, they would get precisely what they deserved for such stupidity. Their infantry would spend the next twenty-five years slogging fruitlessly and harmlessly across the tundra while the rest of the world relaxed. There was as much military strategy in such an idea as in the U.S. suddenly establishing a beachhead on Big Diomede Island. But then, it seems nothing is too fantastic for this military age, so perhaps there was justification for the wariness.

Kotzebue is the home of the Mukluk Telegraph, *The Arctic's Greatest Newspaper*, an accurate brag since it is also the Arctic's Only Newspaper. Its publisher, Gene Joiner, a retired bush pilot, scorns all laws pertaining to slander and libel, especially on the subjects of Archie Ferguson, the CAP (Civil Air Patrol), and the Kotzebue Game Warden. I'm told that a descriptive report of the Warden's recent wedding concluded with the line,"Both friends of the groom attended." Another social note reported that "Archie Ferguson, local windbag and buffoon, is on a visit to Seattle with his combination business partner and mistress." One of Archie's spicy malapropisms is a self-pitying moan when crossed, "I'm gonna have a intergal hermage!"

The Telegraph's "News From the Villages" section attracts correspondents from all of the northern villages with reports on their village activities. The following from Point Lay is typical:

Here I am again visit my friend in Mukluk Telegram program. I haven't got much to tell you, anyway here's my proudest news I am going to tell about.

Edgar Toina winner in dog race on Christmas Holiday, so our school teacher was so proud of him he has to broadcast to Wainwright weather bureau that he like to see winners from there and here have a dog race. So finally, all this Stockholders at Wainwright Native Store was called to up to have annual meeting. Edgar was one to go. Soon as we get there every one start to talk about their dogs would go many miles an hour so the people start putting some prizes in merchandise for winner including three big wolf traps and dog racing flag. This make Edgar wishing to go. It was Jan.13 so next day six teams went against Edgar in 24 mile round trip. Finally Edgar win the race which makes the most people at Wainwright get disappoint.

Many of them are wishing to go to Pt. Lay to have dog race some time. Only thing it was not fair - they never give Edgar the flag, just make him a raggy flag. This make our teacher disappointed. He is wishing to make a better flag for Point Lay, color blue and out of better cloth.

When we got back home men who remain in the village kill some caribou and seals. One feller get one wolf. We have big Eskimo dance for Edgar, our dog race winner at Wainwright. Boy, everyone was happy at the time it make the school room seem very small when everybody lift up their voices in singing and by dancers hollering, children and old folks alike. But still we are disappointed about our raggy flag.

Well, I haven't got much to tell news. We haven't a mail plane since last three weeks. While we were at Wainright the girl was lost by sudden storm hit village, time 7 pm. This is not good news. They haven't find her yet.

We, hope to see you again. Many hello to everyone and God bless you all.

In the late afternoon of our third day in Kotzebue, we were having a needed nap at the hospital. At 5:30, a voice said, "The last boat is leaving at 6 o'clock" At least, that is what I thought a voice said. I was too sleepy to be sure, and the effect was all one in any case. We dashed frantically out and hailed a ride on the fire truck down to the waterfront.

The lost boats, all but the Kobuk, had been sighted five miles off, creeping in at a snail's pace. One tug was towing two tugs and a loaded barge. As soon as they got in, one tug would leave.

It was hours before they reached the beach, and then the batteries were down on the only one in running condition. It had first found the missing tug and loaded barge stuck on a sandbar. Then it had gone to rescue the other tug, which had conked out altogether and was drifting into Siberian waters. Having round-ed up the lost boats and barge, it had towed them all in. All this took about thirty-six hours. This heroic boat's name was Swan. It would wait until daylight and, with charged batteries, start out once more to the North Star. We were stranded for another night. It seemed inadvisable to return to the hospital, which was a half-mile from the loading barge. We felt, in any case, that we had stretched our welcome there.

By now, the daily gathering at the Roadhouse for a hot meal had expanded to include a crew of engineers bound for Cape Lisburne to install a loran system. This is the long-range navigation system in which pulsed signals sent out by two pairs of radio stations are used to determine the geographical position of a ship or an aircraft.

I had an "it's a small world" experience when it turned out their medic had been an orderly at Harborview Hospital in Seattle when Bob was a resident. He had been a guest at a party at my house. We created some raucous commotion that lead to the spilling of several bowls of hot soup by exclaiming with noisy gestures over this astonishing discovery. Doubtless the others wondered what sort of hostess it was who didn't recognize her own guests. It had been a come-and-go party for hospital personnel that lasted most of the night to accommodate all the different shifts. I wouldn't have recognized most of the guests.

A planeload of new arrivals had filled up Mrs. Hanson's rooms. Among these were Dr. Larsen (the archeologist from the University of Copenhagen), his wife, and charming 13-year-old son. It was a privilege to meet them. Unfortunately, they were too weary for much conversation and retired early.

Mrs. Hanson now emerged as a benevolent angel by offering her living room for us to wait in. We had determined to stay within watching distance of the waterfront from now until something went out to the ship, and whatever it was, whenever it was, we intended to be on it. Besides Hazel, Mary Sherman, and me, there were the two nurses from Bethel and two social workers who also had relinquished their rooms and were in like predicament. We crowded into the small living room and began a canasta game to while away the hours ahead. Mrs. Hanson brought cookies and steaming cups of aromatic coffee brewed with eggs. The Larsen's young son, a tall, thin, tow-headed and obviously intelligent youngster played with us until his mother insisted he must go to bed.

Since each of the Kotzebue tugs had been adrift from eight to thirty-six hours at one time or another in the past three days, it seemed wise to pack some kind of food with us so that in case whichever boat we left on followed the pattern, we would not be reduced to imbibing seal oil to stay alive. To this end, the nurses procured two loaves of bread; Mrs. Hanson donated peanut butter and jam, and we prepared sandwiches. They smelled so good it was a temptation to eat them right then.

At this point the two nurses and one of the social workers announced that they had arranged for rooms at Bess's and were going over there to sleep until the boat left. Mrs. Hanson was horrified, insisting that they could not go there! But they were intractable and maintained that the rooms were clean and it was at least a place to stretch out. They left as we called after them a promise to carry back to their stations a report of where they were last seen.

With the arrival of the Larsens, Kotzebue began to seem like the crossroads of the world. Amos Burg, the Norwegian photographer who was traveling with us on the North Star, had wisely retained his room. He turned out to be an old acquaintance of the Larsen's, making for a jolly reunion. It also began to seem that we were abandoned there. Our tempers were short and our nerve ends frayed like King Neptune's rope. For the most part, we didn't talk. Once we started, it was difficult to keep from snapping at each other. We lapsed into a kind of mental numbness. The routine of hoisting gear and preparing to embark, then unloading it and collapsing had been reenacted so many times, that by now it was pure rote.

The canasta game petered out to a lethargic finish. Amos turned in with an alarm clock and promised to get up at 2:30 and investigate the boat situation. Hazel and Mary sprawled on the floor. I took a chair. And the remaining social worker from Nome had the couch. We planned to sleep until hopeful action was reported at the barge.

We slept until, true to his word, at 2:30 Amos came through flashing the beam of a flashlight on us and relaying word that the Swan, certainly the most promising of the tugs, was still half full of water. It would not be ready to leave before seven. The perverse tub that we had come in on originally was going to leave quite soon. But this was also the boat that had drifted over the International Date Line out of U.S. waters the day before, and furthermore, was the smallest and dirtiest of the lot, though none of them were savory by any standards. This one was so obviously a poor risk that we decided to wait on the Swan and went back to sleep.

All of us went back to sleep that is, except Hazel, who for some obscure reason remained posted at the window observing the wharf activity, until, unbeknownst to us, she decided to go down and investigate. At 3 A.M., she woke us up by dashing into the room insisting that the boat was ready to leave immediately and we must hurry. Too nearly asleep to question, we fumbled around for our gear and stumbled downstairs in the dark. As soon as we had scrambled aboard, we realized that this was the very boat we had just decided not to chance. But it was too late. We were on our way.

Only four of us had got into this predicament. The rest were still asleep in Hanson's Hotel or, presumably, at Bess's. There were two crewmen, one who steered with one hand and tinkered with the engine with the other and one who manned the bilge pump vigorously with both hands throughout the trip. By squirming across the engine, it was possible to get into the forward cabin where there were two incredibly filthy bunks, the only places to sit on the entire boat. The wind was high, and I decided I would rather be washed over the stern than to spend hours of a rough ride in that malodorous cabin.

So Hazel and the social worker from Nome crawled forward while Mary and I remained on the cockpit. I say "on," not "in," deliberately. It wasn't really a cockpit. There was no "pit," just the deck with a two-inch rail around the edge. There was one object that by gross exaggeration might have been called a seat. This flat relic, possibly once the seat of a folding chair, was set on an empty gasoline can. By balancing carefully, it was possible to maintain a sort of sitting position on it. We took turns between this contraption and the two-inch ledge of the cockpit. Sitting, or more accurately squatting, on this with our bottoms hanging out over the water, we clung to a coil of tow rope to stay on board. Whenever we soared up a high wave and crashed down the other side, we simply sat in the ocean.

Good fortune was with us for once. The tug's engine pulsed steadily along, never missing a beat. Within an hour, we had sighted the North Star, and no ship ever looked so beautiful. The trip was competed in record time: two and a half hours. We arrived well before breakfast time and were slung aboard in the freight carriage amidst shouts of greeting. The crew had not seen a boat or barge of any variety for forty-eight hours. We had left so unexpectedly in the middle of the night that they had not been informed of our coming. They were as surprised and relieved to see us as we were to see them.

At once, the world began to take on the pleasant aspects of civilization. We breakfasted and then began washing Kotzebue out of our clothes. Sig proffered the crowning gift when he had our shower turned on for one bath apiece. Home never seemed so good nor small amenities so precious.

At noon, the Swan arrived with the rest of the passengers. To our great surprise, the moment they were aboard, we found ourselves underway. Other attempts having failed, it was now up to the North Star to locate and rescue the missing Kobuk. It was reported to be south and drifting helplessly to the west and the dreaded soviet waters. For six hours we searched, backtracking all the way to Shishmareff below the Circle. Finally, we circled back and discovered it safely anchored off Cape Kruzenstern.

The Kobuk and its crew of five Eskimos had been lost now for four days. They had rolled and rocked in a sea growing more turbulent each day. They had an ample supply of seal oil for sustenance. I doubt they would have traded it for filet mignon had they had the chance, but still, they must have been an unhappy crew. A towline was attached to the North Star and we pulled them back to our anchorage off Kotzebue, where the Kobuk was left to find whatever means of getting to shore it could.

This last adventure took place on Saturday, August 26, and that was Skipper's birthday. With much ingenuity, and from the limited materials at hand, we wrapped dozens of useless and foolish gifts, which we'd been collecting for weeks. The ship's baker magnificently frosted the square end of a loaf of bread with bright pink icing on white. In ornate flourishes, it spelled out, "Happy Birthday Captain." We unearthed several of Father Neptune's paddles and with these trimmings surprised him in his quarters.

By the next day, the tugs and barges were back on schedule and the unloading proceeded at a steady pace. At 5 o'clock in the morning on the 29th, the remaining passengers and Bill Wanzer came aboard from the last tug, and we weighed anchor for Wainwright.

CHAPTER 7

Wainwright to Barrow to North Pole

Cruising to Wainwright, we had two days of ideal weather. An azure sky was webbed with shifting cloud formations, and the Arctic Ocean was the cold and sparkling sapphire blue you would hope it might be. At day's end, the sky blazed with fiery sunsets so inexpressibly beautiful and long-lived as to choke the adjectives in one's throat. We were in the land of the seal, the oogruk, the sperm whale, the blue whale, the beluga (white) whale, the walrus, the polar bear, and the true Parky Eskimo.

The North Star's arrival in Wainwright an hour before dinnertime was met with the enthusiasm of a Christmas celebration. Boatloads of people came out to meet us. Those who could not find places in the boats lined the village beach. Some waded out in the water up to the tops of their hip boots or mukluks in an effort to get nearer. Those who reached the ship scrambled up the ladder, their faces alight with grins. A beaming face in a blue and wolverine parka hood shouted happily up at the deck rail, "Hello, Moe! Whadaya know?"

Wainwright was home for the few school children who still remained on board. They lined the deck rail searching for familiar faces and calling greetings to friends and parents. Yet the actual reunions were masterpieces of restraint. A handshake and trembling, grinning faces were all the emotion demonstrated.

The parkas were remarkable: This occasion warranted holiday best. One was made of rich wine-colored corduroy with a lush wolf ruff. Another fabulous one was royal purple chiffon velvet with shirred sleeves and fire engine red trim. The red trim carried through on her mukluks. I asked her how she achieved the red dye to stain the leather. Imagine my astonishment when she replied that she had squeezed it out of wettened red crepe paper! Later, I learned that crepe paper dyeing is common and used often in basket weaving to obtain rich colors.

Underneath the parkas, Eskimos wear anything from flannel pajamas to rayon house dresses, as revealed in the ship's clinic. A common Eskimo substitute for the soap and water not often available to them is a mixture of seal oil and urine. One of the things that most impresses them, when they have occasion to spend time in a hospital, is taking baths in tubs full of warm water. It is of much greater "back fence" interest than details of operations, and it's talked of long after they have returned home.

When we arrived in Wainwright, it was a bright and beautiful evening, but by the time we had been ashore long enough to have coffee at the schoolhouse, a fog had closed in so densely that it was impossible to see the ship anchored less than a mile off shore.

Unloading proceeded rapidly and was finished by breakfast time, even though it slowed down as soon as the foodstuffs were offloaded. Ordinarily, the crew tries to hold back the food until last, after lumber and oil drums have been discharged. The moment the food hits the beach, everyone trots home for a feast. This far north, there are no lightering services, and the cargo is all handled by the Eskimos in their own small boats and umiaks. Some villages don't even have small boats. Then the crew does its own lightering, with the two launches and two barges the North Star carries.

Everything was dragged onto the beach and deposited for later checking and distributing (no warehouse here). When we started back to the ship at 10:30 at night, the fog-bound beach was a strange sight, with hundreds of cartons stacked under a few bald electric light bulbs, while groups of Eskimos sat or wandered about among them.

Wainwright is a village of between 150 and 200 residents. The teachers, the Krowels, husband and wife, her mother who never ventures out of doors or associates with natives, and their two children are its only white residents. Their daughters, aged three and five, were so excited over the oranges and margarine that had come on the ship that they skipped and bubbled and radiated vivacity all over the place. The five-year-old stoutly maintained that she could "smell baked potatoes all the way from Kotzebue."

We encountered authentic sod igloos with the summer tent pitched alongside, as usual. No drying fish here, but scores of animal carcasses hung about the houses and lay on the roofs ripening: caribou, seal, brants, and muskrats. A fifty-foot whale had been killed in Wainwright the year before and supplied the whole village. We sampled real muktuk at the Krowel's home and found it not only palatable but good. However, this muktuk was boiled rather than raw and frozen, as the Eskimos prefer it. And we ate only the skin, disdaining the pink blubber that is an essential part of true muktuk.

A visit to the school's "cold-storage locker" illustrated the completely logical method of refrigeration in the North. It was a deep hole in the ground covered by a frame building, a more sanitary and accessible variation of the "icebox" used by natives. Permafrost maintains the freezing temperature year-round. Cakes of ice cut from a fresh-water lake not far from the village are kept here until they are cracked up and put into an indoor container to melt and become drinking water. It provides an efficient deep freeze, where bread and pastries as well as meat may be stored indefinitely. An Eskimo "locker" is the same, only simplified to a hole in the ground large enough for one man to crawl into.

Wainwright dogs were even more wild and wolfish than those in Kotzebue, although we saw some roly-poly puppies so new their eyes were not quite wide open. Their mother's temper seemed to be softened by maternal pride for she allowed us to examine them closely and even pat them.

During the winter just past, an epidemic of whooping cough had struck Wainwright as well as most of the surrounding villages. There is only the dispensary run by the teachers and what medical consultation can be had over the radio from Dr. Rabeau in Kotzebue. Due to the lack of proper medicines, all of Wainwright's children under two years old were lost to the disease.

Among the half-dozen or so patients nurse Gaddie and Dr. Sherman saw was a girl who had treated a sprained ankle by wrapping it tightly in kerosene-soaked rags. By the time of our visit, enough gangrene had set in to cause her the loss of a big toe. Our visit was fortunate timing for her.

The natives of Wainwright are neat, self-respecting, and cheerful. Even a short time with them gave a glimmer of the reason why many people who live with and write about the Eskimos tend to become overly sentimental about them. Perhaps there is a tinge of envy behind this. To be simply happy, without need of the accessories and complexities that seem so necessary to peo-

135

ple of our historical time and place, is to arouse a grudging and covetous admiration.

Surprisingly, we heard a discordant note from some of the people we met who had at various times worked with the Indians of the Interior and the Aleuts as well as the Eskimos. They contend that, in contrast to other groups of native Alaskans, the Eskimos are vain and prideful people, that while they smile and offer friendly greetings to white people, they thoroughly and fundamentally hate them. If this is true there is a basis for it.

Eskimo culture, like the Polynesian culture, is classified by historian Arnold Toynbee as one of the few extant arrested cultures. It matured early and quickly, probably because of the simplicity of its goal. The single problem confronting the earliest Eskimos was essentially the same problem confronting them today, to wrest and maintain a livelihood out of the cruelest and bleakest of climatic conditions. This is no mean goal and its attainment no mean accomplishment. They did it quickly because they had to or face abrupt extinction. With remarkable ingenuity, they developed weapons and skills enabling them to hunt and kill some of the largest, wildest, and most formidable animals in the world. From their yield, they fed, clothed, and warmed themselves successfully. But having mastered this priority, all their energy was consumed in maintaining that elemental existence. No time and energy was left for curious exploration in supplementary directions. Interestingly, the Polynesian culture was arrested for the exact opposite reason, according to Toynbee. Life was too easy, and posed little motivation for experimentation and invention.

Within easy reach of several of the coastal villages, there are open deposits of an inferior but wholly burnable grade of coal. Through all the centuries of their struggle in the North, the Eskimos never discovered on their own initiative, that heat and light could be obtained from it. Instead, they continued to burn the valuable seal oil which is also their essential food.

The necessity to concentrate their energy on survival and hunting techniques which caused the arrestment of versatility has led them now to an alternative of extinction or assimilation by Western culture, really no alternative at all. Instinct warns of what white people's infiltration signifies, and a people as justly proud as the Eskimo/Inuit, logically would respond to such dismissal with deep-seated resentment.

There is, of course, sufficient reason for bitterness less closely related to primal instincts. Treatment of the Eskimos with the coming of the first white people and the treatment of Indians during the pioneering of the United States have not been dissimilar. The first whites to penetrate the Arctic regions were whalers and fur hunters, and they came armed with superior hunting techniques. They did not have, and did not choose to concern themselves with, the Eskimo's innate understanding of conservation. They accomplished mass slaughter of the animals on which the natives lived. In a relatively short time, the fine fur-bearing animals were all but extinct, and whales were so scarce that starvation for the Eskimos seemed inescapable.

Fortunately, the voracious hunters were followed by men with more altruistic aims, like Sheldon Jackson, who at once saw the plight of the Eskimos and set about to effect some sort of salvation. Jackson fostered the importation of reindeer to Alaska and the development of ranching techniques in reindeer herding. Aided by skilled herdsmen from Lapland who came with the reindeer, the Eskimos learned how to raise them. It has not been easy. Ranching is alien to Eskimo culture, and reindeer moss grows so slowly that the herds must be periodically moved from place to place. But today, the somewhat domesticated reindeer and their wild cousins, the caribou, are important food staples in the North.

When we reached Point Barrow, a short run from Wainwright as distance is counted in Alaska and the farthest north point of our trip, the ship was inundated by crowds of rowdy, egocentric Eskimos, whose personalities appeared in sharp contrast to the pleasant people we had just left in Wainwright. They swarmed over the side of the Star via the Jacob's ladder, babbling to each other shrilly in an unintelligible sounding foreign tongue. All were arrayed in their finest parkas of wild calico prints, no two alike. They raced up and down the decks and companionways, opening doors, smoking carelessly around the oil drums on the afterdeck, and getting into everything like so many vandals, until finally, Skipper and Gaddie, with the aid of most of the crew, were able to corral them and send them packing. During the entire course of the trip, this was the only place where the villagers who came aboard were out of control.

Barrow Village has become a sizable place since the Navy began operation of its base at Point Barrow. Its present population is close to 1,000. Most of the native men are part of the construction crew at the base, where they receive phenomenal salaries, as much as $700 a month. When you consider that actual negotiable currency was practically nonexistent for these people until only a few years ago, you begin to understand some of the social problems created by such wages.

The influx to Barrow is draining other villages. Wainwright, for instance, lost so many families that they were facing the possibility of having the ANS school closed for lack of the required twelve students. An adjustment to such a shift in population would not be so difficult were it not that the boom in Barrow is doubtless temporary.

Another gloomy result of the Barrow fox fire is that while everyone is eagerly grasping at the white-man's paycheck, the unique and exquisite native arts of ivory carving, baleen weaving, and basketry are falling by the wayside. Skin sewing, since it is women's art and necessary to clothe the family, is not suffering so much. Still, that too, may be doomed.

Barrow has an ANS hospital, although its only doctor comes in from the Navy Base for afternoon clinic. He is an Ear Nose and Throat specialist but handles the variety of problems as well as he can. No ANS doctor has been there since Dr. Maisonville left more than a year ago. There were six patients in the hospital, but this is not an indication of a healthy populace. The village of Barrow is ridden with tuberculosis and is without facilities to isolate even the most infectious cases. A nurse told me that for her first two months in Barrow, she cried herself to sleep every night over the uselessness of delivering babies in the antiseptic atmosphere of the hospital delivery room only to send them home to their one-room dwellings and their TB-infected families.

Tuberculosis is indeed Alaska's number one problem. Number one because unless it is defeated, time and expense spent in other directions will have little significance. It seems likely that, short of a full-scale offensive, tuberculosis will be the winner in the struggle for Alaska's natives. It is not enough to take yearly x-rays, count them, and file them. It is not even enough to treat and cure cases in hospitals like Mt. Edgecumbe, Seward, and the prospective one at Anchorage, only to send them home to be reinfected. If we value the future of Alaska's natives at all, we owe them the benefit of all-out war against this devouring disease that came with the encroachment by Europeans..

The energy of the small staff of the hospital is so taxed by the challenge of simple maintenance that there is little left to devote to nursing the sick. A head nurse is burdened with staggering crises of food, housing, freight, and general upkeep. If she keeps her staff and her hospital plant one jump ahead of the rigorous Arctic, she has accomplished a Herculean task, without even touching a hospital's reason for being. Mary Sherman found at least one patient in need of surgery, which she would gladly have performed. The head nurse, Miss Simmons, discouraged the offer because she felt they were not equipped to handle a post-operative patient. It makes a hospital seem like a useless edifice that might just as well not exist.

Lack of potable water presents more hardship in Barrow than anywhere else. The only drinking water comes from ice chopped from a distant lake and stored year-round in an ice cellar. Fresh water for other uses must be carried from a nearer lake at premium cost. This water is dark as asphalt and discolors linens, white uniforms, and stockings to a dirty yellow-brown. The appearance of a tub full of this awful stuff is so disheartening you have to push yourself to get into it.

Seeing these Northern villages during the scant weeks of their summer is to risk passing unfair judgment on them. They are meant to be blanketed under ice and snow. I have no doubt that Barrow is infinitely more bearable to look at with its usual beautifying snow carpet. When the ice and snow vanish, a miserable expanse of mud and debris is revealed. It is not uncommon to lose a boot beyond recovery in the muddy beach. Inland, away from the beach, are fields of tundra, flat spongy land alternating with coarse grass and stagnant puddles. Of course the winter scene will be marred by virtual darkness, relieved, one supposes by brilliant displays of Aurora Borealis.

The graveyard is located some distance behind the village. Because the ground has no substance like ordinary soil and because it is impossible to dig more than a few feet at any time of the year before reaching the impenetrable permafrost, the buried coffins rise to the surface within as short a time as two years, exposing their contents.

Remains of not-too-recently-slaughtered walrus are scattered about in the mud. They are so ripe that even the dogs have lost interest. Here and there, their strange old-man faces gazed up at us with dead eyes from their severed heads.

No trees of even the scrubbiest variety exist here. Last Christmas, the Navy flew in trees for those white families with children, a tremendous treat. One of the teachers said her only requirement for their next transfer was that it be a place with trees.

In good tourist tradition, we engaged a bush pilot named Stengal to fly us out over the point, which is the northernmost spit of land on the North American continent, and over the spot where the monument to Wiley Post and Will Rogers is erected on the desolate tundra where their airplane crashed in 1935. The monument is a granite obelisk bearing a commemorative plaque. It is said that Mrs. Post asked the Eskimo boys who found the wreckage to name what they would like as a gift. Their choice was bicycles, which they received. It is impossible to imagine pedaling a bicycle through the mud and the tundra or over the ice and the snow. No one could figure what use was made of them.

For those too young to remember, Wiley Post was a renowned aviation pioneer having twice set the record for flying around the world. His companion, Will Rogers, was Cowboy Humorist, Radio Commentator, Newspaper Columnist and Author, Movie Star, and Philanthropist. An Oklahoman who was part Cherokee Indian, Rogers was adored in a way and to a degree that arguably no celebrity before or since has been. Their ill-fated flight was described as a survey to find a mail and passenger route from the West Coast to Russia. It has always been supposed that Rogers also had orders from the U.S. State Department for a reconnaissance mission in Soviet Russia.

A bush pilot describes the coastal weather around Barrow as horrible. "The wind comes off the Arctic ice, across the open leads and turns into ice fog. That lays on the ground about 400 feet thick and you dare not enter unless you know exactly where you are going." Post and Rogers did not know the area. They landed on a lagoon near Barrow, where they saw people, to ask directions. One can imagine Post saying, "It's only fifteen miles. We can make it, and then we'll have fuel, a warm bed etc. Let's push on to Barrow and wait there for better weather." Clare Okpeah, an Inuit, saw the plane wreck and ran the fifteen miles to Barrow to report it. When he described the two men to Army Sergeant Stanley Morgan, Morgan knew it must be the two famous travelers. He radioed the War Department and led a recovery party. The whole world mourned the loss of the great flier and the beloved humorist.

While we were sightseeing, the North Star's crew unloaded hundreds of tons of freight onto the beach without benefit of lightering equipment. In four days the task was finished. We sailed away from Point Barrow with never a glimpse of an iceberg or a polar bear to the great disappointment of the "tourists" and the great relief of the Skipper and crew. Sig accommodatingly offered to heave ice cubes over the side so that we might report having seen ice in the Arctic

CHAPTER 8

Point Lay, Point Hope and Kivalina

"Mail Bag!" These are the sweetest words to North Star passengers and crew. Friends and family could use the itinerary created before the ship left Seattle, but dates and ports-of-call change drastically. The whole matter of mail is a haphazard gamble at both ends. The first hurdle for the traveler is to persuade others that a letter addressed to him or her c/o USMS North Star; Kivalina, Alaska, is not tantamount to a letter addressed to St. Nicholas, c/o North Pole.

Mail follows the ship around by air until, with luck, it connects at some port. If out-going letters updating the itinerary are received, they may help, but success is chancy at best. I received an envelope after my return to Mt. Edgecumbe that had zigzagged its way back to the sender and was then forwarded to me as a curiosity. It had been stamped by six different post offices, "Ship left Port. Destination unknown." I felt like a missing person.

It's amazing how quickly mail can get around if it happens to be in the right place, at the right time, and in the right kind of weather. In Pt. Barrow on the first of September, I was handed a letter mailed in Michigan on the twenty-sixth of August. It is equally amazing how thoroughly and ridiculously mail can get snarled and travel around aimlessly for months. A bag of longed-for mail came into Barrow from Fairbanks while we were there. Through a mix-up in the post office, it was flown back to Fairbanks with the outgoing mail on the day we left. Between this mishap and the relatively mild weather that kept us gaining on the schedule, it was October before any great quantity of mail came aboard. Getting no mail cast a pall over everyone. The question, "What do you suppose is happening at home?" "Have they forgotten me?" "Does anyone care?" popped up in almost any conversation.

On the way south, we stopped again briefly at Wainwright where Molly and Beverly, two of the girls we had left there, came aboard eagerly. They were already homesick, both for the ship and for school. Replacing their excitement and anticipation about "getting home," the thought now uppermost in their minds was how quickly could they get back to school. They were still wearing suits and topcoats, disdaining the more practical "parkys" of their friends and families

Blown by an icy wind bitter enough to remind us where we were, we arrived at the isolated village of Point Lay. Last year Point Lay's teachers, newly arrived from the States, had been flown in by early fall and then saw no other airplane for seventeen weeks.

In all of Point Lay, there are just two frame buildings, the schoolhouse and the native store sparsely stocked with food staples, such as baking powder and flour, some buttons, and a few items of clothing. The store was noteworthy for its scrubbed tidiness. Its manager was a pregnant woman close to term. One small parky-clad child clung to her skirt and another to her shoulder.

The first thing we noticed about Point Lay was that the ground was solid — no mud! The second was an almost complete lack of animal traces. This had to mean hunting was poor. Yet the residents of Point Lay depend for existence upon hunting and what few jobs are available at a Coast and Geodetic Station a few miles down the coast. The seventy souls in the village had a meager livelihood indeed.

I had a delightful meeting with an elderly couple, Grandma and Grandpa Johnson. They spoke no English but used their best efforts to carry on a congenial and lively conversation. Grandma wore the black chin tattoo, achieved by rubbing ashes into lacerated skin, which each young girl used to be given when her betrothal was announced, and then carried to her grave. Grandma's generation were almost the last to continue the custom. Today, it is only seen on very old women. She pointed out her "igloo", then, with enviable dignity and pride, said, "Inuit me". Igloo is the Eskimo word for house, and Inuit is the Eskimo word for Eskimo.

Point Lay had no boats of a size to meet the North Star so, for the first time, the ship's launch was put to use. Passengers rode in atop the sacks of coal and cartons of food on the towed barge. As the launch drew too much water to come nearer than several yards from the beach, a line from the barge was heaved to the people waiting on the beach who then towed it in as close as possible. Even so, leaping from barge to beach over the surging surf was a wet and athletic gambit.

The ship's launch gave us a sense of security about ship-to-shore transport, which we never felt in the raffish miscellany of crafts we'd been using. Therefore, it amused us greatly when the launch towing us back to the ship on an otherwise empty barge broke down and went drifting. It happened repeatedly. Each time the launch stopped, the barge swung around at an awkward angle alongside. When the diesel engine started again, the barge would snap about like crack-the-whip. Fun! We boarded the ship chanting a made-up ballad about "A small carousel in the Arctic."

Point Hope was next. With a population of 300, it is located on a geologically fascinating spit of land jutting out from the mainland. The sea keeps it in a constant state of alteration. In its endless pursuit of change and erosion, the ocean washed open the remains of an ancient Inuit village on this spit not long ago. In 1939, it was discovered and named Ipuitak. Its archeological findings are the subject of a monograph by Dr. Larsen and Professor Froelich Rainey published in 1948.

On the basis of their study of artifacts found in the old uncovered igloos, Larsen and Rainey made anthropological conjectures about this northern culture. They found particularly strong correspondences to descriptions in similar studies made in Western Siberia, which lent credence to a belief that the people of Alaska's Arctic regions were originally forced across Bering Strait by pressure from more advanced cultures. The fact that Norton Sound is a dividing line between dialects suggests that the Ipuitak findings, 125 miles north of the Arctic Circle, are representative of the northern Inuit culture and separate that group from the Bering Sea Inuit in the Bristol Bay Area.

Larsen and Rainey surmised that the Ipuitak village dated back to the first or second century A.D., making it older than the Bering Sea culture. Making it, in fact, the oldest site yet discovered in Alaska. This; however, has been discredited since publication of their work, by the intensely interesting process of radiocarbon dating. A count of the carbon-14 atoms in the relics of Ipuitak indicates that they are a little less than 1000 years old.

Whether the remains are 2000 or 1000 years old made very little difference in the fascination they held for us. As soon as we reached the beach, we made a beeline for the Ipuitak site. Our untrained eyes would not have recognized the terrain as anything but an extension of grass-covered mounds, but a little information can give wings to the imagination. The knowledge that we were walking through the homes people lived in a thousand or more years ago made us tread with awe.

Old whalebones littered the ground, especially the huge pancake-shaped vertebrae. We couldn't guess their age, but they were certainly ancient. They provided visible proof that the hunting was once more plentiful than it is today. . When the digging at Ipuitak was finished, the archeologists carried away only specimens critical to their research. Consequently, historically interesting and valuable articles remain that are either duplicates or too imperfect to be useful. These become the property of finders. The Point Hope residents, especially the women, dig industriously in the ruins and sell what they find. It is one of their pitifully few ways to earn money. We squelched the temptation to dig in the mounds for the thrill of finding some artifacts ourselves. It would be unfair for us itinerant tourists to usurp this earning potential; their's, after all, by right of inheritance. In fact, they asked so little for articles that seemed to us fabulous treasures (such as jade knives) that we were almost ashamed to buy them.

Point Hope boasts another unique spot - - its whalebone cemetery. The graveyard is fenced all around by bleached whale ribs, affecting a caricature of a picket fence. Its entrance gate is a pair of jawbones, and all markers, decorations, and memorials are variously shaped whalebones.

Unloading cargo was hampered in Point Hope by the fact that all of the able-bodied men of the village had gone north to Cape Lisburne to work on construction of the radar installation.

All of the long shoring had to be done by ship's crew, women and children. When the launch towing a barge got as close to shore as its draft permitted, the tow line was thrown into a crowd of youngsters who played an uproarious game of tug-of-war with it until the barge scraped bottom. Women working two to a drum in relays rolled the heavy drums off the barges and up the steep slope of the beach while the children lugged cartons, sacks of coal, and other supplies.

Point Hope is one of an increasing number of villages in Alaska where the teachers are Alaska natives. A native's understanding of the educational and social needs of the people can't be equaled by any white teacher. If that can be combined with a background of knowledge adequate to the task, then the native teacher is ideally suited. When schools like Mt. Edgecumbe start their students on the road to real achievement in this direction, they more than justify their existence.

Of course, the demands on teachers in Alaska's outposts are fantastic. In addition to teaching the three R's, they must be doctors, social workers, policemen, engineers, clerical geniuses, cooks and bakers, electricians, radio operators, carpenters-and patient, gracious, and ready to be hospitable to any sudden influx of visitors. These are huge responsibilities for people only scantily trained in most of these fields.

After the first magnificent day in Point Hope, the weather blew up, leaving us with 10,000 pounds to offload and a beach surf making work impossible. We remained idle and at anchor for most of three days, until the weather cleared enough to complete the discharging. During this hiatus, radio communication with Kotzebue informed us that the Flemish Knot, of the Alaska Steamship Company, had arrived there and that the Ferguson tugs and scows had gone into their erratic routine. One had been sent to Cape Lisburne to help unload a supply ship there; it was lost en route. Between the weather and the irresponsible tugs, everything in the area was at a standstill. Ships' captains were commiserating with each other all over the airwaves.

The several stormy days were followed by another day of gorgeous weather for our stop at Kivalina, whose setting is as exquisitely beautiful as its name. Behind the flat tundra colored like golden wheat is the gentle lift of rolling rose-and-purple hills of tundra moss. Beyond these are higher hills of gray and white granite, and visible behind these are jagged, saw-toothed, snow-covered mountain peaks. During the day, the sky shaded from bright blue through all conceivable blends of indigo and lavender. Whenever and wherever you chose to look, the shapes and colors were different from the last time you looked. Around the periphery of this canvas of delicate color were mirages of floating islands.

Just before dinnertime, I looked out of my porthole and was startled to see a flock of brilliant turquoise terns. They were the chalky turquoise you might find in an impressionist painting and so definitively this color that I thought I was seeing some sort of rare arctic bird. I studied them through binoculars with wonderment until one flew out of the reflection of sky and water and became a drab gray gull.

Kivalina is even more poverty stricken than Point Lay, if possible. Here, the greater number of people do not even have parkas. Most of the children were dressed in hand-me-down garments derelict from some corner of Western civilization. The only livelihood is hunting, and hunting is at low ebb. The village does not own a whale gun and harpoon to even attempt to equal Wainwright's minimal record of one whale. Occasionally, they can catch the smaller beluga in nets if they venture into Kivalina's quiet little bay. Hunting is chiefly seal and fish, and even seal is scarce. Since it requires one large seal to make two pairs of mukluks, a woman is hard put to keep her own family in clothing, much less make extras to sell.

For most of the morning, we chatted with Mr. Austin Thomas, a crippled but alert old man. He had mastered excellent spoken English with a keen grasp of the subtleties of idiom. This he had done with no schooling at all, just an obvious love of good talk. He delighted in answering the thousand and one questions we delighted in putting to him. He gave us graphic descriptions of techniques for hunting and fishing and for the dying and bleaching of skins.

Kivalina Eskimos achieve a lovely delicate rust color for their mukluks. According to Mr. Thomas, this is done by chipping willow or alder into fine shavings and boiling them in water for a little less than an hour. The sealskin is dipped while the dye is cooling — "after it is cool enough to put your hands in". Then the skin is carefully stretched to keep the color from becoming darker in the creases. When Mr. Thomas looked at a small pair of children's slippers I had purchased earlier in the day with my "stowaway" in mind (they were a brighter shade than those he wore), he said, "For that color, three handfuls of chips, and the skin is rubbed instead of stretched." Bleaching skins to the white-white used for trim and for the lacings is done by weeks of soaking and scraping in snow and ice, with no bleaching agent used at all.

Fur is removed from the sealskins by soaking them in oil while they are still wet from the sea. After skins have dried, oil soaking has no effect on the fur. This is why seal pokes turned skin side outside carry oil without harming the fur. Caribou and reindeer hides are scraped clean of fur and fat by soaking in cold water. To sharpen their cutting tools, Eskimos use caribou horns to chip off bits of the edges all around until the desired sharpness results.

We asked numerous people the meaning of the euphonious name Kivalina and got as many different answers as people questioned. Mr. Thomas baffled us by drawing in the sand with his crutch a diagram of a house with many rooms and saying that the last room would be Kivalina. An old woman named Edith said the village was named Kivalina because of its location between two rivers, "because it is this side of the other river, or something like that." From all this, we deduced that in some way, it meant the last of a group.

Kivalina was the new station for the Pettits, our co-travelers on the White Mountain expedition. They had left the Star at Kotzebue and flown to Kivalina. A disastrous mishap had temporarily deprived them of their belongings. Their things had been packed the fall before to be delivered from Wales to Kivalina while the Pettits were on their vacation. They expected them to be waiting when they arrived at the new school. The kind of error that so easily occurs in this part of the world thwarted their well-laid plans. The cargo of household goods had been sent instead to Golovin where it was held all summer and put aboard the North Star for delivery to Kivalina. Since there was more than a three-week lapse between the Pettits' arrival by plane and the Star's arrival on its south-bound trip, the Pettits had been stranded all this time without food, bedding, or proper clothing.

They were less badly off than we'd feared. The combination schoolhouse and living quarters, new the year before, was pleasantly modern and attractive. They had borrowed bedding from the outgoing teachers, and for food had ample quantities of caribou, brown bear, bread, and coffee. This made up in nourishment what it lacked in variety. Mr. Pettit greeted us still wearing the straw hat that had served him through the White Mountain downpours.

By now, our sense of values had undergone such profound changes that we took for granted the hazards of the ship's ladder and the bounding small boats that we leapt into and out of in pursuit of jaunts ashore. Before each stop, we found out from Bill

151

Wanzer the quantity of freight to be unloaded and translated this figure into skin-boat loads by ourselves. We estimated the speed with which the skin boats could carry out their work, shuttling from ship to shore. And we were able to evolve for ourselves a reasonably accurate guess as to how long the ship would stay in port.

We had long since discovered that the most satisfactory means of boarding was via the freight sling that had given us such a thrill in Golovin. As the cargo lightened, the North Star rose out of the water. As she rose, the angle of the ladder stair-stepping down the side of her hull became steeper so that it was becoming a breathless climb. Once, when we returned through a rollicking sea in one of the ship's own launches, there was so much turmoil in the water that to bring the launch near enough for its passengers to jump to the ladder would have risked battering it to pieces. The cables were let down, attached, and the launch with a full load of passengers was reeled aboard. This was the least strenuous but the most frightening boarding we made. I found I had more confidence in my own agility, even though it was waning daily, than I had in the strength and reliability of cables and winches.

CHAPTER 9.

Norton Sound "Milk Run"

The scheduled stops on the North Star's route from Point Lay to Teller Mission, a distance of approximately 750 miles, offer not one protected anchorage. Southwest from Bering Strait lies a straight sweep of ocean all the way to New Guinea. Even the strung out Aleutian Islands do not reach far enough West to intervene. And the Bering Sea is so shallow, thanks to the settling sands of Alaska's mighty rivers, that a sudden wind will whip it from a docile friend into a raging, vindictive fiend in no time at all. Luckily for sailors, the reverse is also true. When the wind dies, the friend returns instantly. Too often, though, the wind whistles relentlessly out of Siberia for days on end, and a fifty-mile-an-hour gale is "usual weather." The Star's itinerary allows for much delay during this part of the voyage.

But the Gods of the sea were with us. The water was calm, the sun was brilliant, and the wind almost nil. In ten days, we reached the protection of Teller Mission, having called at Deering, Shishmareff, Wales, and having made one quick stop at Kotzebue to disembark a passenger who'd been suddenly called home. At Kotzebue we found the Flemish Knot still in residence and still having troubles. Only one-third of her cargo had been discharged, and her beleaguered Captain was not hoping to be finished until well into October. This was serious business, for Marine insurance in the arctic becomes invalid after September 23 because of the threat of the ice pack.

Deering was a disappointment; Dr. Larsen's caves were twenty miles inland from the village, and we hadn't time enough to see them. Missing the first launch in the morning turned out to be our good fortune. The launch had difficulty with the long shallows leading to the beach and finally passengers were sent off in a lifeboat to row themselves ashore. When last seen by the crew they were stuck on the bottom and struggling to free themselves.

A later trip on the scow got us ashore without mishap. Deering is a village much under the influence of Western Culture. The men work in the mines in Candle a few miles inland and for twenty years they have been more affluent than most. There's a difference between the people of Deering and those in Barrow where there has been only a year or two of jobs and money. It's the difference, I suppose, of the Nouveau Riche. In Barrow there's a brash, unpleasant easy-come-easy-go atmosphere, while here they seem comfortably independent and stable. They still, though, live in the same squalid huts we saw in Kotzebue.

I was glad to have seen Deering for the attitude of the people seemed to speak a wee bit better for the new influences. It was discouraging to find in village after village the likableness of the Eskimos to be in direct proportion to the smallness of its white population.

Approaching Cape Prince of Wales in the clear weather, we could plainly see the Siberian shoreline as well as King Island and the Diomede Islands. That morning, a four-motored plane with a hammer and sickle on the underside of its wing flew low over us. Although it was not surprising, considering our location, it startled us and caused a litany of speculation to stimulate lunchtime conversation.

The point of Cape Prince of Wales is 348 miles farther west than Honolulu. That this fact is difficult to credit is fostered by the deceptions of the Mercator projection maps of our school days. In Alaska, a mental image of the earth as an orb is essential to grasping the most elementary of geographic relationships. Go look at a globe with this in mind. It will amaze you.

Jagged rocky cliffs form the shoreline of the Cape. Atop the bluff that extends out from the village of Wales is a rock formation called "the weeping widows." Long ago, the legend goes, a handful of hunters from the village went to sea. Their wives kept vigil on the bluff for their return, but they did not come back. The women remained on the high cliff, weeping and watching, until they turned to stone. And there they still are, kneeling, with bowed heads silhouetted against the sky.

Surrounding Teller is a horizon surpassing even Kivalina in its beauty. Teller has the only natural harbor along this coast. It boasts a curving spit of land that forms an almost perfect circle thereby shutting out the wind and heavy seas. Varicolored rolling hills of tundra and mountains are backed by an ever-changing sky displaying sunsets, sunrises, and Aurora Borealis with lavish abandon.

Teller Mission was founded in 1894 by a Lutheran missionary, Toleef Brevig, as a reindeer herding station. If it was not the first in Alaska it was *one* of the first. He was originally requested by the Norwegian Lutheran Synod to leave his post in Minnesota to accompany, as pastor, several families of Norwegian Lapps who were being imported to northern Alaska to teach the Eskimos the art of reindeer herding. Although historical reports vary as always, depending on who is reporting, it appears that the Siberian herdsmen first employed as trainers for the Eskimos were considered barbaric and cruel in their treatment of the reindeer. Five Norwegian Lapp families, one single man, and a youth of eighteen agreed to come to America on the condition they be given a pastor of their own faith to minister to them. The place they came to had been established two years earlier and named the Teller Reindeer Station in honor of the then senator from the state of Oregon. Brevig and his family served there until 1917 managing the reindeer herds and providing a school and shelter for parentless Eskimo children. It was a time when the people of the north were struggling just to stay alive. Diseases brought by white whalers were causing whole villages to simply disappear. An Eskimo friend of mine tells me that the old-timers of his youth said the cold germ caused much of the decimation. "The hot cold germ" they said, "landed on the nose and traveled to the respiratory system clogging it up and killing its victim." That sounds like a good description of pneumonia. Of course it was followed by the even more deadly poxes both chicken and small.

The Teller Mission was a haven and saved lives. It also educated children in its school, teaching them both English and Norwegian so that some of them became accomplished linguists. Though Brevig considered his mission to be that of saving souls, his much greater service was the saving of the lives and dignity of many Inupiat people who would otherwise have been lost entirely. They honored him for this by giving him the name Apaurak meaning "Father of all." An old wise man named Atkutouk said of Brevig, "He came to us long before anyone else even thought of us. He came and helped us when we were sick, and gave us food when we had nothing to eat, even when we were contrary to the God of whom he taught."

EMMA'S STORY

As told to me by her youngest son, William

She was born Emma Neagozook Haggerty. Her mother, Kiahli, was from Agiapak River near Taylor, inland from Teller and Port Clarence Sound. She became the mate of Captain Wm. T. Haggerty and accompanied him on his ship to Herschel Island in the Canadian Arctic where he was sent to establish and exploit the commercialization of ice whales. These were whales that stayed deep in the winter ice rather than migrating south. The whalers had to winter over in order to find them. And Emma was born on the whaling ship at Herschel Island.

Kiahli returned with her infant daughter to her home at Agiapak but she succumbed to one of the imported diseases that were so deadly to Alaska's native people. Before dying she left Emma outside on the gunnichuk (a storehouse built high above ground to keep bears from raiding it.) A hunter came upon the frozen child and threw the blue, lifeless body on his sled in with the fresh killed reindeer that were being taken to the Brevig orphanage at Teller. On the way heat from the reindeer warmed the child's cold body so that when taken from the sled she screamed and scared everyone in the village. They had already been alerted to receive yet another dead body.

A woman of the village said, "Let me have her for the night and if she is dead in the morning I will bring her back to you." By morning Emma was definitely alive but her eyes were still frozen shut. She became a blind orphan under the care of Toleef Brevig, Apaurak.

She was nursed by women of the village and became an inspiration for the people, who thought their whole culture was dying before their eyes. She gave them hope by defying death and living a life without sight, without parents, and being a "half-breed".

Many Eskimos in the villages were half Irish because the whalers left children as well as their devastating diseases. Emma's father offered to take her to Connecticut to be raised by his family. By then she was too much a part of the Teller community to leave. Capt. Haggerty was lost in WW I.

Emma was all right except for her "frozen" vision, and that gave her special gifts of insight. She learned quickly and soon spoke all the languages of the Arctic, as well as English and Norwegian. Through her as interpreter people were able to communicate with each other. She became an excellent reindeer herder because she loved the outdoors, the animals, and camping with the herd. Later she was a moving force in organizing the famous Nome Skin Sewers. She grew up to be a revered wise-woman of the North, and received honors and citations from the U.S. military and President Roosevelt for her valuable assistance during WW II.

EMMA'S STORY

As told by Rev. Brevig in Apaurak in Alaska
by J. W. Johnshoy

On January twenty-ninth a squaw-man brought in a small half-breed girl. She was over a year old. He had found her lying in the snow scantily clad, a short distance outside of Teller as he was on his way home. Close by, the girl's dead mother was lying.

The father was captain of a whaler. An uncle called Spoon, a rather poor character, had taken the little girl and would not give her up. He carried her on his back wherever he went, into saloons and stores. As the little girl was nice and smiling folks gave her food and other articles. But when the people tired of this, and ceased to give, he threw her out into the snow in weather thirty-five degrees below zero.

The squaw-man had passed by a while afterwards and heard the little girl crying. He wrapped her naked body into an old deerskin and drove with her to our mission. Her entire body was blue with cold, and it took a long time before she over came the effects of it.

We called her Emma, in memory of the Rev. R.O. Brandt's daughter Emma, because in a box of clothing sent by Rev. Brandt to the mission were dresses that had been worn by his Emma, which now the little Eskimo girl could wear. The government at Teller would do absolutely nothing to convict Spoon.

Many years later Emma married one of the reindeer herders and the two were faithful members of our mission. The Eskimos very seldom show any outward signs of thankfulness. When Emma and her husband were leaving the mission, she came to us and thanked us profusely for what we had done for her.

These two stories clearly describe the same event. Yet their differences illustrate how much the point of view of the teller influences the version of the tale. It is significant to note that Eskimos have no word or concept for orphan. All the elders in a village are parents to all children. So there really is no such thing as a parentless child.

There are no reindeer at Teller now. They feed entirely on reindeer moss and once the moss is eaten it needs five to ten years to grow enough to nourish a herd. Active stations have to move from time to time. Now camps near Golovin and Mekoryuk are the only reindeer reserves in Alaska.

The Bartletts from Mt. Edgecumbe seemed reasonably well settled and happy with their new school, although they too have suffered from lack of supplies. Their food was on the Flemish Knot still interminably discharging in Kotzebue. We were most of two days in Teller, departing in the evening bathed in one of those indescribable sunsets.

After Teller, we stopped at Nome to pick up what small amount of mail there was. By now, we were two full weeks ahead of schedule, making no one unhappy except that it precluded any chance of ship and letters arriving simultaneously anywhere. This time at Nome we anchored in the company of the Health, a power barge type of craft that travels the coast taking x-rays and offering some general medicine, an Army Transport, and an Army Freighter. After months of being the only ship on the ocean this felt downright cosmopolitan.

All at once, the prepared itinerary began to alter overnight. We would wake up in the mornings anchored in the most unexpected places. The map on which I kept a penciled track looked as though I was sweeping it with a lead broom.

From Nome, instead of moving on around Norton Sound, we took a 24-hour detour to Mekoryuk on Nunivak Island, far south of Hooper Bay. There we loaded 800 butchered reindeer. At Nome we had picked up a small sparrow type of bird. It was terribly lost and confused and hopped pathetically about the deck all the way to Mekoryuk. When the loading began it disappeared. It would have been a long flight from the ship to the shore. We hoped the little fellow made it safely.

Heading back north, we stopped quickly at Tanunak on Nelson Island to unload a mere two tons of freight. We retraced the route between Nome and Mekoryuk in rolling seas, going

160

this time to Golovin, where the reindeer were unloaded and sent upriver to White Mountain.

The White Mountain bomb boat, filled to the brim with school children needing medical attention, put in another appearance and we greeted old friends. Now the weather turned against us. The bomb boat crew spent the night on board the Star while our own crew worked feverishly ashore installing an oil tank for the Golovin School. It was a chill and rainy night, and some of those who spent it ashore brought back a miserable cold that rampaged through the ship during the next weeks. Gaddie stalked about threatening everyone with her needle and syringe full of penicillin until she herself succumbed, subduing her enthusiasm.

Towards mid-morning the tank crew went in again with the oil scow loaded to fill the tank, and we listened in Skipper's office to the conversation between Moe and Sparks. The towline had got caught in the wheel and Mr. Bishop, one of the mates, had to go over the side to untangle it. The engine refused to start and the tide went out leaving them stranded on a bar just off the beach. The wind was beginning to blow and the danger of weather was imminent. After dinner the gas launch went in to rescue them. They all missed both meals that day, chicken for lunch and steak and strawberry shortcake for dinner.

There was autumn and the smell of winter in the air, a different smell and different feeling from the ordinary northern cold, a crisp, clear cleanness.

Before leaving Golovin this time our passenger roster, which had dwindled to six after the stop at Nome, was substantially increased by Mrs. Blatchford and five of her seventeen children. The Blatchfords were an Eskimo family or rather, as Mrs. B. explained often, they were half-breeds. She and her husband were both half white and half Eskimo. And this, she felt, was the cause of all their troubles. And troubles they'd indeed had. The previous winter, the father and one older son had been lost in the loose ice of Golovin Bay while hunting. They had always been a poor family, and the loss of their father left them destitute. Now they were moving to Homer, near Anchorage, where a married daughter would care for them.

Mrs. Blatchford had been born in a village fifteen miles from Golovin, and until she boarded the North Star, her known world extended no farther. She knew it would be a long trip from Golovin to Seward, where she would disembark. She thought it might even take as long as a week. She had, of course, never been aboard a ship, nor had she ever encountered appointments like silverware, menus, and shower baths. The children were, Violet, 14, Charlie and Joe, 9 and 7, and her youngest, twin boys who celebrated their 4th birthday on board. They were beautiful children whose unpredictable behavior added great interest to the succeeding months.

Gaddie, with her usual resourcefulness, rigged harnesses and leashes for the twins to prevent them falling overboard. The two older boys, although they had never encountered bacon, eggs, hot cakes and the like before, lost no time learning how to pack them away in awesome quantities.

Mama, as we were soon calling her, was poised and alert. Although in boarding the North Star she was abruptly thrust into a situation for which nothing in her life had prepared her, she and her children adapted to the new circumstances with speed and aplomb.

Mama B's philosophy was a form of stoic fatalism designed to make her hardships and heartbreaks bearable. In simplest terms it said that, since they were half-breeds, tragedy was their lot in life so she took it with as good grace as she could muster. She enumerated her troubles, but she dwelt on her joys. Six of her seventeen were dead; several from violent causes. A boy, one of an older set of twins, had been lost on the ice when he

162

was six. Another of her boys had been jailed in Nome on a drunk and disorderly charge and was found suspiciously hanged to death in his cell. Several of her daughters had married white men against her good advice. She was sure no good could come of that.

With some disapproval, she read us excerpts from a letter written by a son whom the army had stationed first in Kentucky and currently in Honolulu. The letter announced his intention to marry a Hawaiian girl, and like such a letter from any son to any mother, its intent was to introduce his fiancee. He extolled her virtues, ending in a final bid for acceptance saying, "And, Mama, she's just like us Natives." The line between Mama's eyebrows deepened, and she who had never before been away from Norton Sound tried to visualize the vast social and psychological terrain between Golovin, Kentucky, and Honolulu. She suspected that all was not well with another of her brood.

From Golovin, we went to Unalakleet to begin what Skipper refers to as the "Norton Sound Milk Run." This was an unexpected change of schedule, caused by the news that the Flemish Knot had finally gotten away from Archie and Kotzebue and was headed for Unalakleet. Skipper wanted to get there, finish and leave before it so as not to overtax Unalakleet's meager lightering service. I'd heard about the change before turning in but most of the passengers woke up expecting to be in Elim only to find themselves many miles south. It's exciting even though bewildering not to know where you'll be each morning.

A considerable sea was running, and the little skiff we rode ashore kept taking on water and wetting down the motor so that it never ran more than three minutes without stopping. Each time it stopped, we drifted crosswise in the trough of the swells. When the motor sputtered back to life we turned again head on to the waves and took a terrific buffeting. This was so commonplace that we no longer even interrupted conversation when we heard a motor conking out. Now it was comment-worthy only when we managed to get from one place to another without complications.

Unalakleet is a clean and friendly village. The Swedish Covenant Church has long had a firmly established mission here. It preaches an unrelenting doctrine of, "Cleanliness is next to Godliness." Many a Lapplander who came with the reindeer settled permanently in Unalakleet and probably strengthened the doctrine. The result is by arctic standards a proud industrious community. For some reason, the permafrost that renders the whole north so barren either does not exist or lies deeper here than elsewhere. The growing season makes up for its lack of length in weeks by its twenty-four-hour intensity, and the people here take advantage of it. They grow basketball-sized cabbages and potatoes an Idaho farmer would envy. The tilled ground imparts a loamy good-earth smell in such contrast to the unwholesome sour odor of most Eskimo villages. It didn't feel so much like an alien land.

In her living quarters over the schoolrooms, Miss Jette, the public health field nurse fed us a luncheon of roast pork sandwiches, fresh cabbage salad, fresh cranberry sauce and fresh blueberry cake. The Andersons, the young couple from Pennsylvania who had come as far as Golovin with us, are settled in across the hall from her and bubbling with enthusiasm about their jobs. Mr. Anderson took over Amos to show him around and while we ate, we heard her kindergarten children singing "Old MacDonald Had a Farm" and "The Farmer in the Dell."

Two homes we visited showed us the extremes of Eskimo home life here. The first, where a baby was suffering a severe case of impetigo, had two small rooms. For furniture, there were two cots, the shell of an ancient foot-pedal organ, and a kind of pen with three-foot sides built into a corner and nearly filled with rags and clothes. It seemed to fill a dual pur-pose as bed and closet. In the middle of the floor was a crate filled with wild goose feathers someone was stuffing into flour sacks. There were six young children and no one else at home.

At the other home we paid a distinctly social call. This house, also with two rooms, was clean, orderly and adequately fur-nished including a dining table and chairs. Eskimos have little need for tables. They usually don't observe a family mealtime. When anyone is hungry, she/he takes a strip of dried fish to munch on and continues whatever she/he is doing.

Eskimo hospitality was lavished on us in abundance. Conversation sparkled with humor and enthusiasm. Mrs. Anuruk showed us her family snapshot album. She showed us her skin sewing and intricate fancies, the decorative bands used on parkas and mukluks. Most stunning was one with a full dog team and sled across the center and hunters and seals on either end. For refresh-ment, she served us strips of dried smoked salmon.

Back on the street an old man pointed to the land across the mouth of the Unalakleet River on which the village is located and said that once many years ago, he lived over there in the "other vil-lage." The big sickness came. Most people died and the rest moved away across the river to this place. As he described the sickness, I said, "Small Pox." "No!" he said, "Big Pox!" The native popula-tion of Arctic Alaska was decimated by European diseases brought by the whalers and hunters and by the influenza epidemic of 1918 to a degree, I believe, few white residents today comprehend.

At 1 a.m. on the 26th of September, we left Unalakleet and were anchored off Shaktoolik hours before breakfast. There we became stormbound and remained so for three days. Things come to a dead halt when the ship is stormbound. There is nothing to do but sleep and eat, and everyone fidgets with restlessness, not so much over the inactivity of the moment as the fact that it may last for any number of days. Once the Star spent twenty-one days in

Boxer Bay off St. Lawrence Island waiting for weather fair enough to unload a few hundred pounds of freight.

By now, so much freight was gone and so much of the water supply was used up that the ship drew only about two fathoms. She rocked and rolled at her anchorage. All members of the Blatchford family, except 9-year old Joe, were seasick. It was not a time when anyone's appetite was at its peak. At lunch our waiter, Tommy, without so much as a warning snicker, handed us this menu:

M/S NORTH STAR
C.H. SALENJUS, MASTER

Wednesday,   **9-27-50**

LUNCHEON:

SEAL FLIPPER SALAD

ICE-WORMICELLI SOUP

BBQ REINDEER RUMP STEAKS (CHEF'S CUT)

HARICOT OF CARIBOU

HAUSENPFEFFERED TUNDRA RABBIT

DESSERT:

BELUGA BLUBBER FRAPPE

BEVERAGES:

VINTAGE SEAL OIL

SPARKLING BERINGUNDY

— SIG SUNDT, MAITRE D'

That evening, we listened to a fuzzy broadcast of the Louis versus Charles fight. Although we concentrated hard on the squeaks, bubbles and hisses that came from the speaker, the only thing we knew for sure about the fight was that Charles won by a decision after fifteen rounds.

The next evening, still stormbound, we'd moved back out of shallow water to a calmer location off Besboro Island, about halfway between Shaktoolik and Unalakleet. I was comfortably settled in the social hall with a book when Bill Wanzer announced to me, "You're wanted on the telephone."

This ordinary statement was so clearly absurd that I braced for whatever practical joke was afoot. I followed Bill into the radio shack where Sparks was in one of his interminable ship-to-shore or ship-to-ship conversations. I waited uneasily. Finally Sparks turned from the microphone and said, "Your Old Man wants to speak to you." I said, "That's an unlikely story." Bill W. countered, "What's so unlikely about it? You haven't seen him for a long time have you?"

I was thinking of a smart comeback when Sparks handed me the radiophone and Bob's voice was saying, "Hi, Honey! How are you?"

I was too dumbfounded to talk sense. I must have asked him 10 times how Pixie was. He claims now that everyone in the north teased him about how his wife was more interested in the dog than she was in him. That is, after they had figured out that Pixie was a dog and not a child we had both abandoned. He was in Bethel on the Kuskokuim River in the interior of Alaska on a flying medical business trip.

Despite the vast empty spaces and the small lonely settlements there isn't much privacy in northern Alaska. Everyone communes with everyone else, and when not communing, they eaves drop on all conversations for thousands of miles around.

After my "telephone" conversation, people I met on shore would say, "Oh yes. We heard you on the radio."

I was still in the radio shack when a message came through that the Kobuk had finally capsized and sunk off Cape Lisburne, leaving a freight-loaded barge to drift away and be lost at sea.

When at last the storm clouds lifted and word came that the weather at our next stop, Elim, was fine, we rushed through the last unloading and sent the last X-ray patient puffing down the ship's ladder still putting on his clothes. In the early morning, we reached Elim - only to find the "fine weather" a myth and ourselves confined to another stormbound twenty-four hours.

But it was a Saturday, and the monotony this time was broken by the University of Washington versus the University of Minnesota football game. Just at the beginning of the second half, with Washington ahead 14 to 0, Sparks had to cut off the long-wave band in order to keep a 12:30 ACS schedule for telegrams. We chewed our fingernails down to the knuckles while we waited. At last the radio came back on. The fans were screaming wildly. Washington threw a forward pass. It was intercepted by Minnesota. And the gun went off ending the game. Washington won, 28 to 13.

Sunday dawned a day of bright October weather. The crew went to work, and we went ashore early in the morning. Elim is nestled in a wedge between mountains where the valley slopes down to a nice but small beach. The surrounding hills are covered with trees! Scrubby trees, but trees! I climbed a hill where I could look down on the water as it came roaring and tumbling between craggy rocks. It was beautiful, a little like Southeastern Alaska. On this point high above the ocean was a grassy graveyard with a cluster of freshly whitewashed crosses.

Elim is small, perhaps 150 people. The few houses seem to belie there being even that many. As I strolled through the village toward the beach, the entire populace met me going the other way; some on their way to church but most were going to see the doctor, a much bigger draw this Sunday.

As part of its freight, the Star carries huge tanks for holding the fuel oil for some of the villages. These have to be installed by a half dozen members of the ship's crew under Moe's supervision. It's a hard job, requiring engineering skill and back-breaking labor. And it has to be done while the ship is in port, regardless of the time of day or night or state of the prevailing weather.

So on this sunny Sunday morning, the residents of Elim first paid their respects to the Lady Doctor, and then sought out a vantage point on roofs or stacked oil drums to see and enjoy the erecting of the tanks.

Three things make this tank installation an entertaining show. The first is the same that draws a crowd to watch a steam shovel; fascination with large equipment. Second is the good-humored horseplay of the crew. The audience hardly realizes how efficient they are until the job is done.

When we reached the Elim schoolhouse early in the morning, we found that Moe, like Kilroy, had been there. Plastered on the schoolhouse door, not far from where the tanks were going, was a placard reading, "CECIL C. COLE 'MOE' FOR GOVERNOR. He wears no man's mukluks!" I've no doubt that if citizens under twelve were given the vote, Moe could aspire to any Alaskan office he chose. For the third ingredient of the spectacle is the way the village kids crowd and jostle for position to talk to or work for Moe. He is Hopalong Cassidy, Buck Rogers, yes, and Santa Claus, Alaskan style, rolled into one. Moe always has peanuts and gum in his pockets. But that accounts for only the minutest fraction of his appeal. Most other white visitors carry candy bars and gum, too. It's almost expected. Moe's gifts are honors bestowed. I was almost run down by a herd of little boys racing to the beach to help carry lengths of pipe. They didn't see me at all. "Five cans of peanuts, He said! Five cans of peanuts!" Then there was a proud procession back, two "men" to a pipe.

Mama Blatchford's mother, now old and invalided, lives in Elim. This is where Mama grew up. An eighteen-year-old Blatchford daughter, twin of the boy who was lost on the ice at age six, lives in Moses Point only a few miles distant. She brought her four-month-old baby to Elim, and they held a reunion. Like Unalakleet, Elim is a neat village. Mrs. Blatchford had told me many times how clean the houses were kept here. This was so "even before the white people came," she said. When she was a little girl they were "just poor," had no nice clothes, but they were always "reeeeeel clean!" Her mother made them scrub the floors and wash their clothes. Now-a-days, they have a foolproof system. Each week a committee of two housewives goes from door to door inspecting each house and reporting its condition at an open village meeting. The committee changes every week and rivalry is intense. No one wants to be outshone by a neighbor, and no one wants to be reprimanded. It has the taint of tale bearing, but it works noticeably well.

The Elim teacher, himself an Eskimo, was enmeshed in the knotty problem of enforcing game laws. As teacher and therefore unofficial leader of the village, he was obliged to insist that they be adhered to. The clash between game laws and Eskimos is serious. While the laws originate as part of a sound design for conservation, they are aimed mainly at sportsmen. The dilemma of the Eskimos didn't figure in the lawmakers thinking. Eskimos can hardly live without breaking the game laws. Commonly, when a man kills illegally to feed his family a charitable game warden looks the other way. But situations arise that baffle everyone. For instance, last year in a nearby village one man alone shot and killed twenty-seven caribou. This appeared to be a flagrant violation, and perhaps it was. In any event, the man was forced to pay the piper. But it's also probable that those caribou would have fed 150 people through the winter. It's a matter of record that that village came near starvation during that year.

This incident had dire repercussions. Villagers blamed the teacher for reporting the kill and would have nothing to do with him. He had not in fact been the whistle blower but that was irrelevant. He had to be transferred farther north.

Elim is an example of the unfairness of game laws when applied to individual circumstances. In the spring when the brants fly north, they pass over Elim. All winter long the residents look forward to shooting these ducks. This is their first relief from the stored winter foods of seal, seal oil and caribou. The legal open season on brants is in the fall and in the fall, when they fly south, their route is nowhere near Elim. How should the teacher deal with this? Whose side is he on?

Eskimos have always been conservation conscious, based on their own evaluation of the prevalence of game, and they would be the least likely hunters to indulge in indiscriminate slaughter. It is difficult for them to see the rationale behind these white-man's rules, made by omniscient lawmakers in some unknown place who obviously have not the least conception of or concern for Eskimo existence. To Eskimos this is just another example of the white man's personal animosity toward them, and sews ugly seeds of resentment.

CHAPTER 10

Amazing King Island

When we reached Nome for the second time on October 2, it seemed a major metropolitan center. There were stores, buildings of more than two stories, giant oil tanks, automobiles, and people who spoke our language! There was the accumulated mail of two months and shore leave for the entire crew, a glorious one night to "tie one on." Coincidentally the army was just cleared and ready to vacate Nome, so they were in the throes of farewell parties. The launch made trips to and from shore every four hours, day and night. Although the water was rough and jumping from ladder to launch and launch to ladder was dangerous, those things did not for a moment deter anyone from going.

I shopped. I bought newspapers, magazines, pocket books, and toothbrushes. My most exciting purchase was nine apples flown in from Outside at $ .50 a pound. I would cheerfully have paid $1.50 a pound for them. For weeks there had been no fresh fruit or vegetables aboard ship, except for the Unalakleet cabbages. Sig had ordered lettuce, tomatoes, celery, and oranges to be sent to Nome by air for pick-up on this stop. As it turned out, the perishables were near to perishing and were edible for less than a week. So we gorged happily on gargantuan salads to make sure nothing went to waste. Soon enough, we returned to the starch and protein diet.

Amos spent the day examining the Nome dredges and returned bubbling with enthusiasm and wild statistics. There were three dredges operating in Nome, one of them being the "largest dredge in the world." Before they can dig up the gravel, the permafrost must be thawed down 120 feet to bedrock. The thawing process, said Amos, takes three years. Fortunately what is thawed in one summer doesn't return during the following winter. In a whole summer of labor the dredge moves forward less than half its own length. At this rate the large dredge had seventy-five years of work ahead of it based on just what could be seen from where it stood. And the other two had between twenty-five and fifty years ahead of them. This might be a metaphor for the slow pace of life in the Arctic.

Tragic news from Unalakleet informed us that since our visit a small child had ventured too close to a tethered dog and was mangled and killed. Also that a well-known bush pilot had crashed. Pilot survived with minor injuries but the plane was demolished.

During this brief hiatus Captain Morgan and his wife came on board for a visit. This was the same Stanley Morgan who announced to the world that the airplane carrying Wiley Post and Will Rogers had crashed. Although it was two Eskimo boys who found them, it was Morgan who engineered the search and to whom the report was made. It was he who received the nation's headline credit for locating them. We relaxed in the social hall while Skipper entertained us with more tales from the Byrd Antarctic Expeditions.

The old North Star was an icebreaker. In one of Skipper's

Antarctic anecdotes five dog teams with sleds had been brought across the ice pack to unload the ship's cargo. The teams were driven up to the ship and tied, while the dogs lay down quietly to rest and the crew paused for a meal. All was well and quiet until a lone penguin came promenading sedately across the ice. Forty-five pairs of eyes suspiciously watched his every step. But the unwary penguin continued to come closer until in a flash there were five teams of dogs, sleds, and harnesses in one angry tumultuous scramble. Fur, feathers, and blood flew in every direction. It took the whole afternoon to get them separated, calmed, and rearrested. There are, by the way, no penguins in the Northern Hemisphere.

Nome also meant taking part in the home migration to King Island and Little Diomede Island, the event we had looked forward to with the greatest anticipation. Each spring, as soon as the ice breaks up, all of the King Islanders and most of the Diomeders load themselves and their belongings into their skin boats and move 75 or 100 miles across the Bering Sea to Nome. It is a thirteen hour trip. In Nome they set up camps for the summer selling their exquisite ivory carvings, and offering a glimpse into their primitive existence, to tourists. Their teachers come with them. There would be no object in their staying behind in a deserted village. When Fall comes, the weather is too risky to attempt the return on their own, so the North Star loads them, fur and furnishings, into her hold, now close to empty, and carries them back to their island homes.

While the North Star's crew and passengers enjoyed the sights and refreshments of Nome, the King Islanders and the Diomeders industriously plied their umiaks back and forth between their summer camps and the ship's anchorage, loading their paraphernalia. The miscellany being lifted into the forward hold was beyond credence: radios, batteries, stoves, bedsprings, sleds, endless seal pokes and boxes, brooms, broken chairs, dogs, guitars, and even that wondrous possession, a bicycle.

After all chattel was taken aboard the people, over 200 of them, came paddling up to the ship in the skin boats, forty souls to a boat, and were slung aboard by the freight lift. Last came the boats themselves, five large umiaks and two small ones. People, from infants to ancients, swarmed into the hold, eating, sleeping, gabbling, singing, and playing games. The two groups held themselves aloof from each other. Moralistic in the extreme and hyper-concerned with salvaging their dying culture, the King Islanders shy away from association with the members of any other group. They are particularly cautious about keeping their children from the "evil" influences of the Diomeders and the Nome Eskimos. The Diomeders are apparently divided into two camps, defined loosely as the drinking Diomeders and the non-drinking Diomeders. The two factions are so antagonistic that in Nome they set up separate villages on either side of the King Island camp.

With the King Islanders and the Diomeders stowed and the ship's crew refreshed (or debilitated, depending on how they had deployed their recreation interlude) by two days and a night of comparative freedom from the rigors of the sea, we steamed out of the citified aura of Nome headed for the most alien and remote outpost in all of Alaska.

At intervals during the preceding two months, old-timers on the ship's crew had warned us that we had seen nothing until we saw Alaska's "cliff-dwelling Eskimos." Their tales of houses stacked one above the other and cables tying houses and rocks to the side of a mountain had indeed whetted our curiosity. And they also had sounded suspiciously like classic sailor's yarns meant to bug the eyes of the gullible. But when I was in person scaling the rocks of King Island, I could scarcely believe what my eyes were seeing. If we had not had the rare good fortune to see it on a day that was custom made for photography, I would surely doubt the veracity of my own memory.

The island is a rocky mountain rising sheer out of the ocean. The village, with the Eskimo name Ukivok, is perched about a third of the way up the nearly perpendicular slope. It seems literally to hang there suspended. I have seen towns built on mountainsides where the hills are steep and the houses grow in tiers. Alaska's own capital city, Juneau, is an example of a town grown up instead of out. But nowhere on King Island, from water's edge to mountaintop, is there more than three feet of level ground.

The houses, looking like overgrown packing crates, are constructed on stilts, one above another and very close together, with connecting ladders, short boardwalks, and stairs. The "beach" landing is all sharp, slick boulders. When a skin boat has been guided as far inshore as it will go and securely wedged between rocks, its passengers scramble out onto the rocks and slip and stumble onward and upward for about 200 yards. (They slip and stumble, that is, if they are off-landers like us. The King Islanders seem to have an intuitive knowledge of where to step and how to balance, and their progress is smooth, a marvel to behold.) At this point begins the ascent of a long precipitous stairway ending finally at the schoolhouse, the lowest building in the village. The only entrance to the schoolhouse is through the basement, past the coal bin.

Over this steep climb the King Islanders pack every scrap of the miscellany brought from Nome, as well as their supply of freight from the North Star. Their first action is to toss the soft seal pokes, filled, one supposes with clothes or maybe seal oil, on the rocks between the boat landing and the beginning of the stairway. These soon wedge themselves down between the boulders and manufacture a somewhat more even footing with better traction over the treacherously slippery rocks. Men, women and children alike, bent nearly double from heavy loads, trek up and down and up and down all day long until one wonders that they do not collapse.

The sled dogs, who have been alone on the island throughout the summer, are friendly, well-fed animals compared to other Alaskan malamutes, huskies, and part-wolf breeds. They have eaten birds and grown fat and had sufficient water to drink from a stream that runs down the side of the mountain. They have missed human companionship, though, and are cloying in their affectionate pleasure at the return of their two-legged partners.

The last and highest structure in the village is the church and the abode of Father Tom. This is a Catholic community and the beloved Father Tom speaks their language so fluently that the King Islanders find it necessary to use English only in the schoolroom. Most of the oldsters and the littlest children do not speak English at all, which complicates progress for the teachers in the primary grades. Beyond Father Tom's home, the mountain extends upward for a good mile. At the top, on the only plateau on the island, stands a statue of Christ, erected according to inscription in 1904. Here also is the graveyard where caskets are covered with piles of rock. Imagine the grueling experience of a funeral procession!

As we climbed toward the top of the mountain, we looked back often to the impressive sight of the North Star quietly at anchor far away and far below us. A thick wall of fog commenced to roll slowly westward across the Bering Sea and we determined to turn back as soon as it shrouded the ship. But its progress halted and it hung there midway like a gray blanket behind the ship's outline.

Children ran wild over the rocks like little mountain goats, leaping and skipping and scaling what looked like bald precipices so quickly and agilely they scarcely seemed human. While they played these hair-raising games of human fly, they shouted to each other in their half-guttural half-clucking tongue that even Violet Blatchford could not understand. An Irishman would believe he had found a leprechaun lair.

It's been suggested, and sounds reasonable, that a possible explanation for the King Islander's persistence in the seasonal exodus is the will to protect their children from the broken limbs that would result from a summer of daredevil feats. The severity of the winter curtails activity to a degree. They play on the cliff with sleds built on one runner like a wide ski. The slope is so steep that coming straight down would put them on loose ice and part way to Nome. So they've found a way to zigzag. King Island must be a massive, magnificent ski slope in the winter. Once Father Tom, coming out of his house at the top of the village, slipped and fell at his doorstep. He slid between the houses all the way down to the schoolhouse roof where he checked his descent by grabbing the chimney before he whizzed past.

The puzzle of King Island is what conceivable spark of an idea could have persuaded the first person who looked at that uninhabitable mountain of rock that hanging a village there was even a remote possibility. There's no discoverable answer to that conundrum, but whoever he was, he must have been a considerable engineer.

Reasons for its continued habitation are clearer. Hunting is excellent. A strong and continuous current keeps the floating icebergs milling and changing in the water at the foot of the island. The sought-after animals of the north that ride about on the bergs are thus brought to the King Islanders, sparing them the trouble of going out on long hunting trips. They can almost shoot seal, walrus, and polar bear from their front porches. Walrus are abundant and important since they supply the ivory for the superior carving the people do.

Another reason for clinging to the mountainside is that such an unapproachable location offers the best weapon to protect their people from encroachments of the outside world. True, Western culture has inserted an opening wedge in the form of teachers. But the King Islanders are accepting this with mixed gratitude. They still steadfastly refuse to send any of their young people as students to Mt. Edgecumbe. One King Island child is a patient in the Mt. Edgecumbe hospital. Perhaps this is another wedge.

Doorless and windowless, the backs of the houses face north and inland. Snow sliding down the mountain piles up against them all winter long. In front, they have small doors, about the size of a window. The sills are set two feet up from porch level to keep wind and snow from sweeping in. The doors are carefully designed to barely admit an adult wearing outdoor winter dress.

An opportunity came to visit the icehouse, and I snatched it. It turned out to be the most strenuous adventure of the entire trip. The icehouse is a cave cleft in the side of the island. At this time of the year, before the freeze, it's reachable only by small boat. Outside the cave the water was placid enough, but where it flowed through the narrow opening it became a tidal rush. It swished and heaved violently, battering the boat against the rocks. Executing a landing inside the cave was a touch-and-go proposition. It took all five of us trying to find handgrips on the rocks to halt the boat as it bounded between them. Finally we quieted the boat enough to get out. We dragged it out of the water and up onto the rocks to forestall its being washed away by the sucking current while we explored. Then we faced an upward struggle over rocks and boulders many times more daunting than those on the beach. Coated with moss and seaweed they were slipperier than wet ice cubes. In places the footholds or hand-holds were farther apart than my legs would stretch. Had it not been for the strong helping hands of the two crewmembers and the King Island and Diomede teachers, all strong young men who were the other four members of the party, I should never have made it. I was ashamed of having to be hauled up the side of a rock unable to give even a boost to relieve my dead weight. But retreat was not an option.

Once over the rocks and onto a small space of level ground, we came to the entrance to the first of the "refrigerators," a hole in the cave wall just large enough for a man to crawl through on his stomach. The hole was kept covered by an oil drum to discourage dogs, for it was not beyond their ability to wander in here. None of us was tempted into this hole, but a flashlight revealed a labyrinthine series of caverns, ledges, more holes, more caverns and more ledges for as far back as we could see. Because of its accessibility to the dogs, this was not used for important food storage.

The second and more utilized "refrigerator" was high above this one and required climbing two long ladders to another ledge. Once reached, it was much the same, though a little cleaner because the dogs had not dragged scraps of over-ripe meat around the entrance as they had below.

Of course, it was not yet cold enough in the cave to freeze any meat stored there, and since there had been no one home for several months, it was not presently in use except for remnants from the previous winter. The King Island teacher was inspecting it to determine whether or not he should try to bring in a buck he had shot. He decided wisely to postpone his meat storage until the arrival of ice and snow. I think one would have to develop a mighty hunger for meat before venturing in after it, and then be sure to take out a supply to last for a long time.

Descent to the boat did not seem nearly so difficult. I accomplished it almost unaided by sitting down on the wet rocks and sliding. I was glad that I wasn't lugging fifty pounds of fresh meat.

In 1951, the year following my visit, Juan Muñoz and his wife, artist Rie Muñoz accepted the challenge of spending a winter as teachers at Ukivok Village. A happy result is Rie's unique and delightfully evocative paintings of village life of which some appear in these pages and Juan's photography, which provide a rare visual chronicle of winter life on King Island. In his article in the January 1954, National Geographic Juan's description of the ice cave wonderfully fulfills my desire to know what that cave was like in winter.

> With the advent of longer daylight hours in March, Rie and I often went for walks after school hours in search of new spots of interest. One of these walks took us to a big ice cave where the villagers store meat.We entered through the mouth, which is well over 200 feet high, and dropped down into an immense chamber. A dim light glowed in the far corner of the cavern. As we approached it, we found an Eskimo woman huddled beside a lantern, getting meat for the family dinner. She was greatly pleased to see us, as was every King Islander whenever we showed an interest in learning more about island ways, and offered to show us around. We went from chamber to chamber, climbing over narrow ledges and up and down ladders, all the while stumbling over frozen chunks of meat. Our guide explained that each family had its own storage place. To us there seemed little separation of the personal caches, for the caverns and paths were literally paved with frozen walrus cuts.I marveled at the enormous supply of meat in the cave. The villagers always keep more that a year's supply on hand, to tide them over in case of a poor hunting season.
>
> — Juan Muñoz, 1954

Winter here brings complete isolation. No planes can land because the ice in front of the island is loose and floating. The year before, during a pneumonia epidemic, which followed a measles epidemic, an army plane flew over and dropped desperately needed penicillin. After the North Star departs, no other means of receiving supplies exists. The teachers were a young and peppy couple, both graduates of Ivy League universities.

This would be their second year on the island. They considered their major problem to be teaching English to the thirty beginning students when they have no common language.

After unloading the residents the freight landing shifted to the other side of the island where they unloaded 100 or more drums of oil. We clambered to this spot to catch the next boat back to the ship. Since we had to wait for a boat to come in and be unloaded, we sat for a long time on now cold rocks and watched the slow task. Drums were loaded about twenty to an umiak pulled in as close as possible and then lifted and rolled by hand up from the water over boards and logs laid across the rocks.

Had I been harboring any notions about my own intrepidness, they were dispelled when I learned that the teachers at both King Island and Little Diomede were expecting babies during the winter, with no more attention available than the native midwives and radio communication with the Kotzebue Hospital.

Homeward Bound

Next morning I awoke with a strained back and aching legs and considered them a small price to pay for having seen King Island. From where the North Star was anchored I could have flipped a pebble out of my porthole into tomorrow and into the USSR. We were almost exactly on the International Date Line, which runs between Russia's Big Diomede and the U.S.'s Little Diomede. Three miles of water separate the two islands. The villages are both on the western sides of their respective islands, so that all we could see of Russia was the barren back of Big Diomede. We were told that a supply ship had visited during the summer, so presumably people were still there. In past years, people of the two villages exchanged visits to trade goods and gossip. In fact there are a number of familial relations between them. But the last time the Little Diomeders went to call, one of their young men was held and questioned for thirty days. With tension mounting between the two parent countries, visits have stopped.

Little Diomede is physically as isolated as King Island, though nothing like so steeply inaccessible. But its people seem a good deal more worldly. They speak beautiful English and, like the family we met in Kotzebue, are bright and attractive. They are better traveled than most Eskimos. They spend summers roving the mainland coast. Also they are good businessmen. Their ivory carving brings higher prices than their competitors, partly because of the quality of the ivory. Little Diomede has quantities of very old and fossil ivory, which is distinctively colored, and more highly prized than new ivory, and their work shows skill and imaginative design.

A shortage of women is distressing the community. The men had fanned out over the mainland during the summer looking for wives but they'd not had much success. Little Diomede, it seems, is too much an outpost for the lasses of the mainland tundra. Mrs. Blatchford, to her delighted amusement, had no less than three proposals of marriage during the few short hours we were in port.

Little Diomede's new teachers are recently married. She is Eskimo and a graduate of the University of Alaska. He had been an army sergeant stationed in Nome, where they met. They'd adopted her 4-year-old sister since both her parents were dead. During the whole of the previous winter, the radio at Little Diomede was out of commission. Thus the only link to their remote neighbors was lost to them for bleak month after bleak month. The thought of such exile is scary. Radio is the one redeeming feature of the lonely northern winter. Still as I watched this couple, I had no qualms about their ability to withstand the hardship and carve a happy life for themselves. They would share wholeheartedly the life of the village, and the benefits would be mutual.

We took on a Diomede youth, an army veteran, bound for Mt. Edgecumbe School. He was a skillful ivory carver, one of five Alaskan boys selected a year or so before to work with William Sprattling in his experimental jewelry project in San Antonio, Texas. We prevailed on the ship's chief engineer to provide tools for him to work with while aboard ship. He carved a pair of earrings for Dr. Sherman to match a necklace she had purchased. Her necklace and also one I'd bought, were made by his brother whose technique, he said, was unmistakable, and the earrings, when done, were a perfect match.

Next stops after Little Diomede were Gambell and Savoonga on St. Lawrence Island. We dropped anchor at Gambell during the closing plays of the Washington vs UCLA football game, which had been an absorbing thriller. It was a jolt to return from the vivid mental image of the beautiful University of Washington Stadium, packed with cheering crowds, marching bands, and a victorious team, to a ship swarming with parky-clad Eskimos.

The weather was foul and small boats were just barely able to make it out to begin the unloading. But each boat brought a horde of people all clutching sacks of carved ivory they hoped to sell. With few exceptions they were not nearly such skillful artisans as the King Islanders and the Diomeders. Much of it was poor to mediocre.

St. Lawrence people are distinctly Siberian and their language is different from anything we'd heard. To my ears it was also unpleasant. They are soft-spoken people, hardly speaking above a whisper. It is a gargley sound that originates in the back of the throat and sounds more like a perpetual throat clearing than a conversation.

Their parkas are different too. Hoods are trimmed with black-dyed rabbit fur and make a tight round frame for the face. When not worn as hoods, they are fastened tightly around the neck and muffle the wearer's face almost up to the nose.

Nautical superstition strictly prohibits whistling on shipboard for dread of "whistling up a gale." At St. Lawrence Island, some lubber must have whistled all the way around the deck. Before the unloading was completed at Gambell, a wind came up. The beach got dirty. Then our anchorage got dirty. And we ran for shelter to Boxer Bay. Skipper calls Boxer Bay the "parking lot of St. Lawrence." It is about a four-hour run from Gambell around the west side of the island toward Russia and provides the only protection for miles. It was named for the old Boxer, a historic ship of the Alaska run predecessor to the North Star I and the first ship to discover its comforting shelter. This was an apprehensive time for everyone, for it was in Boxer Bay that the North Star had once idled for twenty-one days waiting for a break in the weather.

Four Gambell citizens and the public health nurse were stranded aboard with us. For the nurse it made a pleasant and unexpected holiday. But the Gambellites, especially the lone woman, were miserable. I got an indelible lesson in the prerogatives of taste as I watched her face while she tried doggedly to eat Sig's excellent cuisine. I would wear exactly such an expression were I presented with a menu of whale blubber and seal oil, or starvation.

On the third stormbound day the skies cleared but the sea remained wild and the temperature low. To burn some of their pent-up energy, the crew lowered a lifeboat and went ashore to fish fruitlessly in a nearby stream. Boxer Bay's a pretty place with offshore rock formations looking like Crater Lake's Wizard Island and Phantom Ship. Each night it snowed a little in the mountains that rimmed the horizon. And each morning it looked as though an airplane had flown over scattering flour.

Twenty-four hours later there was enough improvement for us to return to Gambell, finish discharging, and take aboard ten young people bound for Mt. Edgecumbe. These excited youngsters had been dressed, packed, and standing on the beach expecting to leave momentarily ever since Saturday. The four

Gambell residents who had been marooned with us were welcomed home as if they'd just returned from a sabbatical in Europe.

We sailed on to Savoonga, and there the Blatchford twins celebrated their fourth birthday. There was ice cream and cake for dinner. Gaddie dug deep in her bag of tricks and came up with two garish little Alaska caps with red feathers stuck in them. Moe and some of the officers furnished a red tissue wrapped basket full of candy bars and gum. The crew took up a collection amounting to over $52. The twin's eyes lit up when the candy appeared and four hands shot out swiftly. But Mama was swifter, and the red paper was folded over the candy pronto.

The money did not make so large an impression on either twin, although one remarked in a satisfactorily overwhelmed tone, "Oh my! Ten Cents!" But the box of silver and folding money brought the same look to Mama's eyes as the candy did to the twins'. For all their toughness, sailors are a kindly compassionate lot.

Leaving St. Lawrence we moved southeast across Bristol Bay toward Dutch Harbor, at last getting some distance from the Siberian border. The weather was not violent, but the ocean heaved steadily with hearty swells. The ship was now nearly without ballast, having discharged her freight and used up her water supply, so that we wallowed through the waves.

For three full days and nights the rolling was so steady and predictable that we grew accustomed to it and went about ship's routine without missing a beat. It was not until a few hours out of Dutch Harbor, when we reached calm waters, that we were aware of the physical strain of moving about and trying to remain upright on a rocking ship, calling into service a whole new set of muscles.

At 11 o'clock on a rainy black night we came into Dutch. I stood on an outside deck and peered into the murk to pick out the lights of that port. To my profound surprise, there were tears welling over and spilling down my cheeks. Subconsciously, as we had left that friendly port-of-call in our wake, I had been uncertain that I would ever again be that near home. It was absurd that this distant, deserted Aleutian post should have symbolized the security of things known, but I felt more of the lift of homecoming that dark night as the North Star slipped up to the Dutch Harbor dock than on the morning some weeks later when I woke to the familiar landmarks of the Sitka channel. Perhaps it was only the knowledge that from now on there would be an abundance of running water and hot showers on demand.

While we were still tied up to the Dutch Harbor dock, a whirlwind Aleutian storm broke, and we remained there for two days until it wore itself out. According to the timetable, we were not due in Mt. Edgecumbe for another three weeks. We had several brief Aleutian stops scheduled, primarily to pick up passengers, for now we were rapidly gathering students to take to school. We also had a little freight for some Kodiak Island ports and would go into Seward to disembark the Blatchfords.

After the Dutch Harbor storm the weather was serene. We whistled through stops with such speed that often we did not even get ashore for sightseeing. In any case we had seen and done so much that all was now anticlimactic. I, at least, was homeward bound and suffering a mega attack of channel fever.

With the passenger roster increasing daily, the atmosphere in the ship seemed to alter. At times we felt like strangers who could not possibly have been calling this home for the past three months. The freshman students we took aboard were alien and unsure, in sharp contrast to the somewhat rowdy and sophisticated group with whom we had begun the trip. They were painfully shy. They suffered seasickness in varying degrees. Meals at regular intervals were strange to them, as were knives, forks, and spoons, and, in fact, the food put before them. In the orthopedic wing of the Mt. Edgecumbe Hospital cod-liver oil is the treat of the day for the young patients.

Many people are mystified to discover that coastal Eskimos, who are inherently a sea-going race, should be afflicted with sea-sickness. To me this is no mystery. I share their contradiction. Rough water in a small, low boat when it splashes over your head or over the foredeck and cabin presents quite a different sensation from that experienced in a large ship. On the ship you scarcely see the water. You feel that you are in a room, on a floor, surrounded by four walls and a ceiling, and like the room of a house, it ought by rights to stay upright, if not stationary. It is distinctly upsetting when the room begins to pitch and toss and drop out from under you. In the very act of boarding a small boat, one prepares for a roughing, but unless you have spent more of your life at sea than on land, this is not true of boarding a ship, and no amount of logical argument will make it so. If you are one of the lucky ones whose balance is disturbed by nothing, I envy you. But the surprised and seasick Eskimo has my warm sympathy and empathy.

As you move north and west, you come to a tree line, just as when climbing a mountain. The tree line bisects Kodiak Island. The southwest half of Kodiak Island is Aleutian in terrain, rocky and barren of trees. But the northeastern half is lushly forested. At Ousinkie, not far from the city of Kodiak, we saw, for the first time since leaving Sitka, trees in abundance, mongrel pet dogs in abundance, chickens, cats, and real gardens. It was an unimaginable relief.

We zipped through the rest of the itinerary, every day bringing home closer, while the landscape transformed rapidly into familiar mountainous, forested shorelines. The Blatchfords and many of the students were up at the crack of dawn with their noses flattened against the window of the social hall. They emitted wondrous and disbelieving sounds. Over and over again we heard the awed exclamation, "First time I see a tree!"

We, of course, reacted typically with amusement and quick sympathy by thinking, "How strange and pathetically wonderful, a child of 18, a grown woman of 50, who has never seen a tree!" At once, though, we were brought up short by the realization of how few weeks ago we had expressed our equivalent of, "First time I see a beluga!" or. "First time I see an umiak!" And what after all is so marvelous about trees or mountains if you are accustomed to living where you do not have them to cut off your view of distant horizons?

We sailed up Resurrection Bay to Seward and I could not get my fill of gazing at the majestic, rugged mountains of the Kenai Peninsula. They are among the most impressive peaks in the world. At Seward the dazed Blatchfords got off, still wearing fur and calico parkas, and looking out of place. They were met by someone who took them off quickly to Homer. Most of us spent the two hours in port gawking at civilization, lunching in restaurants, and staring at well-stocked department store and grocery counters.

I had anticipated seeing a school chum of mine from college days in Michigan. Fran and her husband, Per Osmer, had been living in Seward where he worked as a longshoreman. I didn't have to go far on the dock to find out about them. To my disappointment I was told that they had moved to Clam Gulch still on the Kenai Peninsula but some miles from Seward. Later when I complained to Fran that Clam Gulch wasn't on any map so where in the world were they, she informed me that it wasn't on the map because she and Per were putting it there. They were the town of Clam Gulch.

We hastened back aboard the ship happy in the knowledge that only two days in the Gulf of Alaska stood between us and Mt. Edgecumbe. We left Seward-and then the storm struck. This time the Gulf lived up to its reputation. The lightly loaded ship ploughed head-on into the wind. She was reduced to a scant two knots an hour, and there was no Boxer Bay to run to.

I took to my bunk not daring to move from it for fear of falling or being fallen on by some dislodged object. We might use up all of the time we'd gained just weathering the elements in the Gulf.

On the night of the third day of this beating I went to sleep supposing that we were still somewhere in the middle of that infinite, raging Gulf making less that two knots an hour and doomed for days on end to put up with the interminable pounding.

The first thin rays of light filtered through my porthole and woke me out of a sound and restful sleep. There was a quiet and serenity about the ship. Perhaps Skipper had found a Boxer Bay after all. I got up, almost for the first time in three days, looked out the porthole, and behold, broadside to my vision was Old Sitka Rocks! Its dependable, unfaltering light blinked at me through the morning fog saying, "Welcome home, weary traveler. We've been waiting for you. You're just in time for Thanksgiving."

EPILOGUE

On the day after Christmas, at 9 o'clock in the morning, the Stowaway opened violet-blue eyes, the shade of Alaska's skies, and introduced herself to the world as a dainty, ruddy cherub named Barbara Rose. The first thing she saw was a modern chrome and white delivery room. Two doctors and two nurses hovered over her to make sure her every need or demand was expedited. Six more doctors and a whole hospital full of nurses and attendants tiptoed outside the door and in nearby corridors straining their ears to hear her first vocal pronouncement.

The ninth, and most concerned, doctor had been dispatched an hour or so before to the diet kitchen to boil 20 gallons of water one quart at a time.

No baby was ever ushered into the chaos of separate human existence with more expert professional attention. There were lung specialists to make sure she breathed properly, bone specialists to make sure her arms and legs were all there and straight, internists to see that her inner organs functioned correctly, and fifty trained persons who would have run to her aid at the drop of a stethoscope. Not that she required any such solicitude. All she wished to do was howl a lusty, "Hi, Mom. When do we eat?"

But I found my stateside friends awed by my courage and stamina to have my baby born in Alaska. Oh yes, they'd heard that I had made a trip somewhere before she was born. But think of having a baby in a place like that! I should write a book, they said. Explanation was useless. So I wrote a book.

When she was four months old, Barbara Rose made another trip on the North Star. This time she was accompanied by both Mommy and Daddy. Her destination was Seattle. And from there to points east, including Chicago, to meet Dr. Mary Sherman. Daddy proudly passed out belated cigars to officers and crew from "Barbara 'Polar Bear' Shuler, who stowed away on the Barrow trip."

She loved the ship and slept contentedly in her basket believing that it rocked exclusively for her. Nor was she non-plussed by the roar of civilization: airplanes, trains, and highway traffic.

Not so her parents. The hurly-burly of city life was terrifying. Hurtling along a highway at the hair-raising speed of fifty miles an hour brought my heart into my throat. Never before had I realized how much implicit trust we put in our fellow humans each time we get into an automobile. When we come to crossroads with stop signs, we assume the other will stop and we speed confidently on our way. It doesn't occur to us that if he or she chose not to stop or was an Eskimo who couldn't read English, it might be the last trust we ever placed in anyone. I felt safer leaping from a ship's ladder into a bouncing umiak.

Before our two months of vacation ended, old habits had returned, and the task of coping with civilization did not seem insurmountable. Yet it was a joy at last to step off the DC-4 at the Juneau Airport en route to Sitka, and drink in the cool, sweet-smelling Alaska air. Mountains soared a stone's throw away and rivers of mist spilled down their rocky eternal slopes and enveloped us in a silky film of homecoming.

AFTERWORD

Fifty years is a large enough container to hold a lot of change. From this vantage point, I know more about some of the players in this story. Just a year or two after my trip, the North Star II gave way to an even larger ship, the North Star III. She was a converted liberty ship, and her skipper was none other than Cecil C. "Moe" Cole. Moe had first gone to sea as a dishwasher on the Boxer in 1937. North Star III continued to serve coastal Alaska until 1984 when she was decommissioned, much to the very vocal dismay of those for whom she was still a beloved lifeline. A North Star and her sturdy, loyal crew had made over 120 trips on the Alaska run, two trips to Antarctica, served the US military during WWII, and been the recipient of many honors and commendations.

"Sparks" is the nickname given to ship's radio officers all over the English-speaking world. Our "Sparks" was Roger Darby who was serving his second year in that position when I was a passenger. As far as I know he stayed with the ship until she was decommissioned. One midnight above the Arctic Circle, he and I were leaning on the deck railing watching the endlessly fascinating activity of unloading freight. He had noticed the

Michigan return address on one of my letters. There in the middle of an Arctic night, afloat on the Bering Sea, we made the astonishing discovery that we had grown up in towns less than 20 miles apart. We were so near the same age that we knew people and places in common. These "small world" life encounters never cease to astound me.

Reader's have expressed a desire to know more about my traveling companions, Hazel Ivy and Mary Sherman in particular. Both Hazel and Mary were highly skilled medical professionals, specializing in orthopedics. Hazel was a cracker-jack surgical nurse-technician who assisted Dr. Philip Moore, Mt. Edgecumbe's Orthopedic Surgeon. Mary was on the staff of the University of Chicago's Bobs Roberts Pediatric Hospital where some of Mt. Edgecumbe's orthopedic cases were sent when they needed more complex care than was available in Alaska.

Mary and Hazel shared a stateroom. And I'm afraid as the boss's wife I received special treatment being given the only single passenger stateroom on the ship. I really didn't do anything to earn that perk, but since I liked to use my typewriter to record the day's events it was probably fortuitous.

I don't know their ages, but I'd guess mid or late thirties. Hazel may have been older but she didn't seem so. I was twenty-eight. In any case we were a good trio and the three of us together doubtless plotted more adventures than one of us alone would have. Hazel had been in Alaska for years so in the beginning she knew the North Star crew better than either Mary or I did. Hazel, I'm sure, is the initial reason the three of us were on such buddy terms with Captain Salenjus and Sig Sundt, the chief steward. We each provided a bottle of our preferred alcoholic beverage (scotch in my case) which Skipper kept for us, and each evening we had a before dinner cocktail hour in his quarters. This was special privilege indeed. Owing to my condition, I was not into relishing much imbibing, but I did enjoy the camaraderie and the ritual and wouldn't have missed it for anything.

While we were still anchored at Barrow the US Navy's ice-breaker Burton Island also came into port. We, Mary, Hazel and I, met several of the young officers and invited them to join us for dinner on the North Star. They were thrilled, first that we would feel free to invite them confidently without checking with the ship for permission. (We did, of course, ask permission but we had no doubt they would be welcome and asked only after they had accepted.) And then they could not get over the easy, friendly relationship we all enjoyed aboard the Star. Their captain was evidently a martinet because they continually expressed their envy at the bantering and friendly give and take. They were agog that we talked to the Captain like a real person, and even more so that the Captain was pleased to entertain them as guests.

Needless to say the invitation was not returned although we would have enjoyed seeing their ship and I'm sure they would have enjoyed showing us. They were, in fact, apologetic about not being able to return the favor. I have to say that given the restrictions of ship-board life and the harshness of the assignment it seems sad to me that a crew should not be allowed more freedom to let off steam. The atmosphere on a ship is dictated by the personality of its captain. Salenjus was great. His authority was clearly absolute, respected and adhered to by passengers and crew alike, but no one feared him. It's not hard too imagine what kind of a Skipper his successor, Moe, made.

As happens when people travel together in close proximity for a lengthy period, the three of us occasionally got testy with each other. But this was minimal and each of us seemed to deal with irritation by retreating into silence or going off alone rather than snapping at each other. I took this for granted then, but now that I look back on it I think perhaps it was remarkable.

Hazel, like any good Alaskan loved the natural magnificence

of land and sea and was always up for any excursion so I saw a lot of her as long as I lived in Mt. Edgecumbe. Sadly, just a few years after the trip, Hazel suffered a fatal heart attack and Alaska lost a loving loyal friend.

She was an integral part of the medical team and her untimely death was a terrible shock. She was assisting in surgery mid-operation when she had the sudden heart attack. She said, "Chief, I think I'm dying!" Chief was Dr. Moore. She couldn't have been in better hands and in a better place for an emergency but the coronary was so severe that the doctors who were also her dear close friends could not save her. I have to suppose now that it was because she smoked. We all did. And we all pay a price for that indulgence. Hazel's, though was the worst.

Father Ossorgin left the Orthodox priesthood. He did this gradually, discarding his flowing black robes and long beard and hair a bit at a time. Until this transition began his life had been so cloistered and structured that he had essentially missed the ordinary stages of growing up. It was as though we, his friends, watched him experience in a matter of months the natural discoveries common to teen years including falling in love. He met it all with such wonder and delight that we felt blessed to watch his transformation. He married a young hospital technician and eventually left Alaska to become a professor of mathematics and music at St. John's University.

The dilapidated Baranof Castle was torn down and removed. In its place on Castle Hill is a park commemorating the bloodless transfer of Alaska from Russia to America in 1867. Each year, a reenactment of that event occurs on the 18th of October, Alaska Day. (One summer day not so long ago, I was sitting on a bench on Castle Hill reflecting and reminiscing, gazing out over the Sitka Channel with its hundreds of birthday-cake islands to the volcanic peak of Mt. Edgecumbe and beyond. I was joined by a couple from one of the many luxury cruise ships that now regularly visit Sitka. After awhile, the man turned to me and said, "Until this moment I thought that the Bay of Naples was the most beautiful sight in the world." I know what he meant.

Today Alaska Air Lines' jets do land on the Mt. Edgecumbe airstrip. No longer are the PBY and the Gruman Goose the only means other than boat of reaching Sitka. Today a bridge connects the City of Sitka to the community of Mt. Edgecumbe. The shore boats, like so much else, are only a memory

Some of the coastal villages of the North, such as Pt. Hope and Elephant Point, have had to move their locations due to erosion from the sea. This is not new. In the past, rampant disease also forced whole villages to relocate. Shishmareff and perhaps Kivalina are presently facing the necessity of moving. As civilization encroaches, moving towns becomes an ever more complex and costly operation.

And King Island! The island is still there in the Bering Sea, 40 miles west of Cape Douglas, south of Wales and 90 miles from Nome, but no village is there. No people hunt and carve and dance there. No children play leprechaun on its rocky cliffs. Beginning in the 1950s, fewer and fewer residents returned to the island after the summers in Nome until finally by 1970, no one lived there at all. Now there is a permanent King Island Village in Nome.

But the story is not so simple as it sounds. The people were probably right in trying to keep their way of life protected from outside forces. Of course it was a losing effort. The Bureau of Indian Affairs condemned the school and forced the move to Nome, by finally locking the island, warning that "a huge rock was going to roll down, crushing the schoolhouse and the homes in its path." The rock has never rolled down, but the people are gone.

To learn more about the life of the King Islanders, I recommend a book published by the CIRI Foundation in Anchorage called A Place for Winter. Paul Tiulana, whose story it is, simply and eloquently describes the bewilderment of the native people trying to reconcile themselves to modern society. Mr.Tiulana says, "When the government first came into the villages, Native people did not have any lawyers, state troopers, policemen, jails or correctional centers. The government told us we required these agencies, which were not required before. I did not see any child abuse in our village when I was young. We did not have any alcohol or drug problems when I was young. We did not have divorces. We could integrate both systems if the government sat down with us and made plans to educate our children the modern way and the village way, to satisfy both sides. The teachers must sit down with us, and the lawyers and the state troopers and the policemen, and all the other government officials. And we can make a contribution to modern American society." By "sit down with" I believe Mr. Tiulana means listen, respect, and learn as well as advise, patronize and dictate.

The question that nagged me about King Island never stopped nagging. How did they happen to decide to live in that forbidding place in the beginning? I tried to find myths and legends that might give clues to an answer. Somewhere I heard a charmingly plausible tale that during the migration east along the presumed "land bridge," a young couple broke taboos displeasing the tribe so much that they were exiled and left to fend for themselves on what became King Island. It's a temptation to go with this neat Adam-and-Eve explanation but it's more than likely apocryphal.

My friend William Willoya, whose father was an orphaned King Island child, spent much of his youth listening intently to stories told by his parents and their friends. He tells me that without exception they said, "We were always here. We were not walkers over the Bering Strait. We are sea people of the Pacific. We did not move. The land moved."

Willy has spent much of an interesting life pondering this same question, "Who are the King Island people and how did they get there?" He has come to some startling conclusions that although not part of mainstream thinking may not be as far-fetched as they sound. The shifting of earth's tectonic plates has the Pacific plate turning counterclockwise and pushing the North American plate, so that over millennia, it moved west and north, finally creating the landscape that is Alaska today. The people now known as Inuit or Eskimo, Tlingit, and Haida, whatever and wherever they may have been in the evolutionary chain, moved with the land. Those who stayed behind became the Maoris. He has found the traditional legends to be much the same between the native people of the Northwest, the Southwest and the South Pacific, suggesting that all of them are really the mysterious Anasazi. "In other words," says Willy, "we never left our islands ever. Those ancient volcanoes just kept pushing us North. My Ma and Pa and the other elders said over and over, around count-less fires after hunting seals and whales and walrus and birds, that we were a tropical island people! These ancient words have been told to generations as they evolved with the planet during its formative years, getting a free ride throughout the vast Pacific to become the Eskimos of modern times!"

Improbable as this idea may sound, it is scarcely less proba-ble than the fact of the life the King Islanders lived. And, now that I think about it, the picture of Ukivok Village clinging to the side of the Island does bear an uncanny resemblance to the pueblo villages of the Anasazi carved into rock cliffs in Arizona, New Mexico, and Utah.

Finally, I must talk about Kotzebue. My sojourn there, while interesting, was anything but inspiring. I painted a bleak picture with little hope for any sort of brightening future. Although I have never revisited Kotzebue and probably will not, I have studied Kotzebue today via the miracle of the Internet. (For isolated places like much of Alaska, the "information highway" is truly a revolutionary tool.)

The passing of the Alaska Native Claims Settlement Act (ANCSA) in 1971 significantly changed the face of Alaska, especially the far North. Thanks to crude oil and the pipeline, it put money in staggering amounts into the hands of people whose lifestyle had never included serious money.

One hears a good deal about the Northern natives' misuse of the huge sums of money they came into. Especially one hears about the toll that alcohol and drugs have taken on the Eskimos. This is sad but scarcely surprising. Thousands of years of survival living close to nature in a communal society is not a useful classroom for learning to how to deal wisely with unrestricted access to the materialistic Western world full of comforts, luxuries, gadgets, goodies, and anything else that money will buy. Hopefully, generations to follow will not be so overwhelmed.

But in Kotzebue, something so remarkable evolved that the rest of the 21st Century world could profit from studying it and its mission. Wise heads considered how best to use the ANCSA riches for the welfare of the residents of Northwest Alaska. By working together, they combined the Inupiaq understanding of sharing and social living with the wealth the land claims lavished on them, to create an awesome health and social services organization called The Maniilaq Association. Its history and complete description can be found on its impressive web page, www.maniilaq.org.

A picture of the 80,000 square foot, $50 million, state-of-the-art hospital and health facility juxtaposed to my pathetic-looking picture of the Kotzebue Hospital decorated with empty oil drums makes a profoundly positive statement.

I feel a need to apologize to Kotzebue for my pessimistic evaluation of its probable future. I can think of no better way to do that than to share the "Statement of Core Values and Beliefs" established as a standard of behavior for board, employees and clients of Maniilaq Health Services. These values come straight from the needs and the way of life of the Northwest Eskimos to the technology and big business of the modern world. I can only wish that corporations large and small all over the world would adopt, post, and live by appropriate variations of this Maniilaq statement:

> We believe that change is not only inevitable, but presents us with opportunities for improvement and growth.
>
> We will work together to continually improve all that we do.
>
> We will promote an environment of openness, trust and integrity.
>
> We will respect confidentiality for all.
>
> We will be concerned and caring and treat everyone with respect and dignity.
>
> We will celebrate diversity while promoting harmony and self-respect.
>
> We believe work should be fun and fulfilling.
>
> We strive to be fair and consistent in our dealings with others.
>
> We believe in taking responsibility for our actions.
>
> As ambassadors for Maniilaq, we will strive to be a good example for others.
>
> We believe in preserving and promoting Inupiaq values and culture.
>
> We believe that all employees can excel and we will support the development of their full potential.
>
> We believe our best decisions are guided by fact rather than opinions.
>
> We will provide a safe and healthy work environment.
>
> We will support the assumption of individual responsibility through sharing knowledge and skills.

In 1950 I probably caught the Kotzebue and Barrow communities at the worst moment of their transition. It had already visibly begun. They were discovering western money, food, mores etc. They were, perhaps like children "feeling their oats," without the tempering of mature and experienced judgment. Thus my less than enthusiastic evaluation. I pretty much saw them as en route to destruction. I tended to blame the white man's influence, although it was clear that some aspects of western culture were genuinely trying to help. Largely though, I saw in them the future and it didn't look pretty to me.

Interestingly in the smaller villages what I saw was more of the true Eskimo spirit. Survival, respect for others and respect for nature, a gift for living well and happily with what life offered. I envied this and deplored the carelessness and rowdiness of Barrow and Kotzebue natives. I remember being troubled in Sitka and Mt. Edgecumbe by the natives seeming disrespect for property. This, of course, has been a bumpy part of the relationship between the European settlers on the North American Continent and its aboriginal peoples from the beginning, the acquisition and possession of property as opposed to the sharing and non-ownership of the gifts of the land. In one of our plays a Native American was given the deed to a piece of property. Bewildered, he says, "They said it was land! But what good was it? When a man offered me a good knife and a saddle for the piece of paper I took it. The land doesn't have four corners! I have always worked with the horses." Hovick unpublished in 1950.

What I see, taking a really careful look at Eskimo culture is a caring and sharing people who take whatever is offered, be it poverty or wealth, hardship or ease, and make the most they can of it. It's an attitude that might help save the world. A hazard is the bugaboo of population growth. Eskimos are still sharing what is now enormous wealth among a relative few. The first pioneers and the founders of the U.S. were also few in number compared to the natural wealth of the continent. They needed "caring and sharing" to survive. This is surely an important reason for the fine ideals upon which this nation was founded.

A man I admired greatly, Robert Ramsay, who was Dean and Registrar of Olivet College when I was a student there, cautioned us to "guard against those things in the world that may take vitality and harness it; that may take honesty and turn it insensibly into hypocrisy; that will take freedom and give you in exchange order and regimentation. There is something attractive about order. It's comfortable. Freedom isn't comfortable, because it implies responsibility. You have to deserve freedom if you are to have it. It ain't easy, boys and girls." he said to us. "But it's worth having!" He was right. It is harder and harder to "be responsible" and hold on to freedom. And this is also the dilemma of Alaska's native people.

There is no doubt that the "white-man's" culture and attitude were cruel to Alaska's natives as they were to the native Americans of the south forty-eight. It brought not only disease, unhealthy dietary changes, and alcohol abuse but a basic disrespect for the cultural history of the native people, and an arrogant assurance that "white-man's" laws were beyond reproach. Although many people of Western culture prize native crafts and artifacts, the people themselves are often considered primitive and somehow inferior. Perhaps this is inevitable when a more technologically advanced civilization encounters an indigenous one. One has little trouble imagining how we would appear to visitors from somewhere in space. Should this ever happen let us pray that they will be far enough advanced socially to view us with a more open and welcoming mind than we have viewed others in our explorative encounters.

APPENDIX

EXCERPTS FROM LETTERS TO MY FAMILY
IN MICHIGAN

Dutch Harbor, August 16, 1950. Onboard The North Star II
Dear Folks,

My last letter to you I left with Bob unsealed so that he might put in a check to cover the cost of the suit you sent me. It will serve me very well. Thanks. Since our finances were in an abysmal hole when I left, and Bob was to take off for Mt. McKinley on Tuesday; yesterday, I have no idea whether or not he will have mailed it to you.

Our itinerary has undergone considerable change from the one I sent you, thanks to the delay in starting and the addition of several stops of which this, Dutch Harbor, is one. Hooper Bay next on our list is another. I shall try to correct a copy from the one posted in the social hall and send it on to you, although if you add a day or two to the arrival time at each place on the old one you'll probably be very nearly right.

The five-day voyage across the Gulf of Alaska was remarkably easy for that notorious body of water. We rolled steadily but not violently, as is often the case. Yesterday morning we came inside through the Shumagin Islands, the beginning of the Aleutian chain and were favored with a magnificent sunshiny morning, millpond water, and fascinating and astounding scenery. These mountain islands rise sheer out of the sea and although geologically too new to have many trees, they are covered with emerald green grasses and low shrubbery. Where they become too high for even the grass to grow the rocks are a delicate rosy hue quite like the peaks of the Colorado Rockies

By the time we'd gotten out on deck after breakfast, Mt. Pavlof, our first sight of an active volcano, was about forty miles behind us. It was shrouded in heavy clouds, but they kept shifting enough for us to see it spouting curls and puffs of black smoke every three minutes. In fact Hazel, Mary Sherman, and I spent the entire morning on the wheelhouse deck watching this phenomenon through binoculars. I could not resist taking pictures; but, I doubt that even I will be able to distinguish the explosions from the clouds.

By afternoon we were back out into open water again with nothing between us and Australia and we hit the roughest weather so far. I presume this is nothing compared to what we are in for later; but, it took me by surprise and unfortified with Dramamine so that I had a miserable attack of mal-de-mer and did not enjoy myself at all until about eight o'clock in the evening when the Dramamine kicked in and settled me down. I hope this does not happen many times, for it's no fun, believe me.

After batting the question back and forth for twenty-four hours we had finally decided to stop briefly at Akutan to let off a school teacher couple, but when we sailed past the entrance to Akutan Bay at about 10:30 a violent willawaw whistled across the bow of the ship and we plowed straight on for Dutch Harbor.

We docked here at about 6 a.m., our last dock, by the way on the rest of the northern trek, and began unloading 800 drums of oil. Thanks to the tenseness of the international situation we are not allowed to go ashore. That means we cannot go to Unalaska some miles on around the Bay. It is raining dismally and blowing quite gale, and these miles of boarded up glum looking barracks are anything but a pretty sight. Where there were once 60,000 men there are now six or eight, so they say. I don't know why the restrictions on going ashore. All the activity I've been able to see from the deck is two pick up trucks and three men I do not identify as members of our own crew. Dr. Sherman was called into Unalaska to attend to medical needs there, and perhaps she'll be able to tell us more about the lay of the land and what goes on. This is, of course, a submarine base. But from our disadvantageous point of view it's impossible to guess where they might harbor any submarines. We can see the airstrip from the ship, but it puzzles me how there could ever have been much air activity in such a windy spot. In any case on a day like this it is not difficult see why the men stationed in the Aleutians during the war were unhappy with their lot.

From here on, until we get into the Arctic Ocean, we are in the Bering Sea. This is our last opportunity to take on water, so we shall be rigorously restricted from this point on. Showers will have to go and there will be no doing laundry.

Of the thirty-nine passengers aboard at least half are school children and patients from Mt. Edgecumbe who will get off at Golovin and be returned to their respective homes. Four of us are round trippers, Hazel Ivy (x-ray technician), Dr. Mary Sherman (Orthopedic Surgeon), Amos Berg (world traveler and photographer), and myself. One other nurse (Carolyn Briedig) from Edgecumbe is going only as far as Golovin and flying back from there. The remainder of the passengers are teachers going to the various villages. One young couple fresh out of college are on their way to Unalakleet. Another couple with two children have been a year in Metlakatla and are going to Mountain Village. She is quiet and charming, but his qualifications for teaching are twelve years as a sailor and four years in the army. One wonders. The Bartletts, a well-liked family from Edgecumbe are going to Teller Mission.

Probably I shall not be able to get this into the mail here, for I think the mailbag has already gone to Unalaska, but at least it will be ready to go out at Hooper Bay. This promises to be a rugged but most interesting trip.

P.S. Must append a few corrections. First the messy weather lifted at noon and revealed quite beautiful surroundings, although the place still has the desolate look of any deserted military base, It seems the true reason we are not allowed ashore is that previous ship's crews and passengers, notably Coast Guard, have vandalized the valuable equipment left by the Navy and stored in the multitudinous warehouses. With only six marines and two standard oil employees in the entire place there is no one to guard from marauders. We are about to leave so I must hie me up to the deck and watch proceedings.

Sept. 24, 1950. Golovin:

We're back in Golovin again, having jogged from Nome down to Mekoryuk on Nunivak Island where we loaded 800 reindeer carcasses, and over to Tanunak on Nelson Island. From here we make the stops around Norton Sound, Elim next, Shaktoolik, Unalakleet, St. Michael, and back to Nome. I'll mail this letter at Unalakleet. We are still way ahead of schedule and it begins to look as thought we may stay that way. Skipper expects to be back to Nome by the first or second and should not take longer than three days there. I hope this doesn't make me miss more mail for I haven't had much, thanks to the way we've raced through itinerary, Were it not for your letters I would feel

208

very blue indeed. You have had exceptional luck connecting with us all along. I hear nothing from Bob, but doubtless the next Nome stop will remedy that. Here in Golovin Max Penrod, who is director of education for the Native Service came aboard overnight. He used to be our next-door neighbor in Edgecumbe until he took over this new job and moved to Juneau. He has seen Bob recently and expects to see him next week in Edgecumbe so at least I know he is still alive and healthy. There is a good deal going on there in the way of big medical and educational conferences, and the Lion's Club Carnival coming up. I suppose that in addition to the difficulty of keeping up with the North Star he has had his hands too full for letter writing.

After Nome you had better write to me first at Unalakleet, and then at Ousinkie. After we leave Nome, there will be no mail in or out until we get back to Unalaska, The islands are the most isolated spots in all of Alaska. They do not even get planes more than once or twice a year when the weather happens to break just right. Their only link is the radio. Last winter the radio on King Island was out of commission during the entire freeze-up. Can you imagine anything more desperately isolated? And yet, the teachers are back there to spend another year. They are a young couple who came up here directly after they graduated from college, he from Dartmouth and she from Vassar. It's hard to imagine anything more taxing to a relationship? What a harsh proving ground. It does often exact a severe toll on marriages.

There is some trouble filling vacancies up here now because people look on the map to see what they are contracting for and as soon as they discover the proximity to Russia they withdraw their applications. I find this ridiculous. Once you have seen this country the likelihood of invasion by anyone at all seems highly remote. The Russians cannot be stupid enough not to recognize it as a fool's mission. If they are going to occupy anything in Alaska they'll surely skip over all this tundra and go directly to

Fairbanks or Anchorage. The chance of being cut off from supplies is not a threat to the people who live here because they are cut off anyway and automatically lay in more than ample supplies for a year.

Much to everyone's relief, excepting possibly Hazel who is always up for adventure, we've had definite word that we do not have to go to Amchitka, Adak, Attu, or any other of the distant Aleutian stations that threatened us for a while. It makes me feel worlds easier because I would have had to leave the ship and fly home. Much as, like Hazel, I would enjoy further exploration that side trip would put me way too close to term to take the risk.

Incidentally, I'm enjoying the navy blue dress. I probably did not sound properly enthusiastic when I thanked you for it because at that time the thought of all that increase in size was so repellant to me that I did not feel very gay about any clothes prospects. But now I am quite used to the new figure and it delights me to look as unpregnant as possible. I can't decide, though, whether it's better to have people think I'm gaining this weight through self-indulgence in the wonderful meals, or have them aware that I have legitimate excuse. I'm not enthusiastic about either option.

Regrettably I have had to forego some side trips; A trip to the graveyards in Barrow and out to the Navy Base because riding for miles across the tundra in a weasel given my condition was not recommended. I felt frustrated and annoyed, but both Mary and Hazel assured me after their excursion that I was wise to stay home. They did not enjoy the jouncing, and were glad not to have to worry about me.

In spite of the fascinations of the trip you could not have mention peaches at a time to catch me in a more susceptible frame of mind. We've been out of fresh fruit and salad stuff since before we got to Barrow and never in my life have I so craved fruit. I thought I might get some apples in Nome, but then we didn't make it ashore. It turned out there were no apples there anyway. No planes and no ships. Sig hopes to get a new supply of greens and fruit on the next Nome stop so in another ten days things may look up. You've no idea how much I appreciate Southern Michigan's fruit, this far away from it.

September 25, 1950. Unalakleet

I left this letter in the typewriter thinking I had several more days to work on it before getting to Unalakleet. There was a sudden unheralded change in plans last night and we awoke this morning in Unalakleet instead of Elim as expected. Now I don't know where we're headed and I've missed finishing and mailing the letter in favor of spending the day ashore. It will have to wait and go out in Nome.

Unalakleet is the nicest, cleanest and most genuinely friendly village we've visited thus far. It was one of the first places they brought the reindeer for cultivation in Alaska and several of the old Lap families who came with those first deer still live there. The Swedish Covenant Mission has been in full force there for years and years, and while they have some drawbacks, as do all mission programs in Alaska, they are responsible for the comparative cleanliness.

I finally got a letter from Bob. He is no longer so disturbed about the Army, having become philosophical about it and deciding that if they start drafting him in a rush he'll join the Navy instead. Meanwhile Dr. Googe and Dr. Haldeman are working on a hurry-up Public Health appointment for him with reassignment to Mt. Edgecumbe for the "duration," whatever that means. If this is effected soon enough it should quell the Army's threats. The bad thing is that it looks as though he may go to Washington for the budget conference the end of October meaning he might not be there when I get back. But that's not too awful and a look at the inner working of the Dept. of Interior might make some of their endless red tape a bit more comprehensible.

October 2, 1950. Nome, Alaska

You need not worry further about clothes. I feel a little ashamed to have made those requests, which must have sounded urgent. I'm not badly off at all. I made by hand, a smock with some material I had the foresight to bring along, and the maternity slacks you sent are a real boon. I was just getting a little panicky about the weight gain and ashamed of myself for not having the will power to eat less. I was trying to restrict myself to a total of fifteen pounds for the whole nine months and find that I have gained ten since coming aboard the North Star. That's what was distressing me. I honestly think I can lose again once I get back to my own cooking, which is not designed to fuel a hard working freighter crew. Bob says that the total weight of a baby and accessory tissues is fourteen and a half pounds and that anything more is going to some unnecessary place. That's what I was trying to avoid. Plus I don't want to get unwieldy before this trip ends and be a nuisance to everyone, or an eyesore for that matter. I know Mary Sherman is an orthopedist and wants nothing to do with obstetrics. I didn't mind using her presence on the trip to help persuade several doctors to rubberstamp my going and to reassure you. But I emphatically don't want to burden her with any responsibility.

Right after I mailed your letter I was astounded to get a phone call over the ship's radio from Bob in Bethel. We talked back a forth for about ten minutes with the whole arctic listening in. Now everywhere I go people say "oh yes, we heard you on the radio." He had planned to fly over to Nome with his bush pilot, Tosh, and spend a couple of days with me there. That would have been a staggering surprise. It feels to me as though

I'm on different planet from the rest of you. But he has to hasten on to Anchorage to see about the Public Health Commission that may save him from the army's clutches, and then to Juneau to show the ropes to his new assistant. He's had a pretty harassing time. Dr. Googe was transferred out of his post as Area Medical Director two months ago. He still has not been replaced and Bob has added Acting Director to his other responsibilities in the interim. Most of this month three doctors, members of an ENT team who are taking care of the school kids and patients, have been staying at the house. Two new staff doctors have arrived since I left in addition to the new administrative assistant. Without doubt things have been hectic. No wonder he's not a great letter-writer. I'm just as happy to be peacefully away from jangling telephones and dinner guests for a while.

We don't have any milk, being now much too far away from a source of supply. But I have been from the beginning taking enough calcium capsules to cover amply the pregnancy needs, also vitamins in sufficient quantity. It was all so scientifically figured out that I shouldn't be surprised if I could get along healthfully with no ordinary food at all. It's just that the food tastes so good.

I do feel a diminishment of stamina. It takes a lot of energy and agility to clamber up and down the ship's ladders and to leap from the launches to the beach and scramble back on again. Not to mention walking through the mud and tundra. Also I persist in eating too much no matter how hard I try not to. I must often seem downright craven to my table companions.

I discovered that Sparks, our radio operator, grew up in Bridgeman. Do you know any Darby's?

Thanks again for all the mail and packages. I'll try to get off another letter before we leave Nome, but I don't want to miss being on deck when the King Islanders and Diomeders start coming aboard with all their paraphernalia.

CHILD OF UNCLE SAM

The 49th Star

By Loel Shuler

The top of the world from a tired czar,
Honestly bought without battle scar,
Called by the Aleuts "Alaksu,"
The congressmen said, "Any name will do.
The land will be known as 'Seward's Folly',
A frozen waste, vast and melancholy."
This being all that their ears could hear,
They neglected Alaska year after year.
And he who sponsored the purchase price
Was laughed to scorn for buying ice.

States that were slaughtering one another
Could not look out for a northern brother.
So God and man withdrew their laws

And Alaska writhed in the looters claws,
Gamblers, schemers, adventurers,
Murderous greed, and the lust for furs.
Pribilof fur seals gathered their millions,
While sea otters joyfully played with their young ones.
The foxes bred, and the martens and beaver.
And death consumed them like plagues of fever.
No law protected. No law controlled
The hunter's aim and the trader's gold.

No one came northward to explore
Except in summer along the shore.
To thrust far inland nobody dared.
To stay and build here nobody cared.
But they found in the waters a wealth of fish,
And the traders again grew quickly rich.
They spread the coastline's sweep to fame
As a place that abounded in fish and game.
But dark still covered the midnight sun,
And Alaska's dawn had not begun.

What of the people who'd owned this land?
The Haida and Tlingit and Tsimshian?
Craftsmen, fishermen, proud and strong
They wanted the strangers to move along.

More friendly, the Aleuts out on the chain
And inured to invasion, did not complain.
They'd worked for Baranof and learned the way
The Russians had taught to live and pray.

From Kodiak Island north to Barrow
The Eskimos hid by a glare of snow

Stayed for awhile in cold seclusion,
Till pirating whalers brought disillusion.

Inland where valleys and rivers flow
The Athapascans were last to know
The staggering forces set in motion
By white-sailed ships that crossed the ocean.
At last came steps in a kinder direction
Lead by builders of school and mission.
We bow in respect to courageous teachers
Who had to be doctors, policemen and preachers,
And the hardiest sort of pioneers
In the roughest and rawest of all frontiers.
They suffered the hardships to reap the joys
Of lighting lamps for her girls and boys.
And who can say they are not repaid
By towers now rising on bricks they laid?

Then! Eighteen-hundred-and-ninety-seven!
The headlines trumpeted MANNA FROM HEAVEN.
The steamer Portland, the story told
Hauled into Seattle "a ton of gold."
And now, as the image of El Dorado
Alaska discovered a new desperado.
As hordes of the Earth poured in to quest
For riches hid in the Northland's breast.

They swarmed in her rivers, and mobbed on her trails.
And flooded her town sites with wild wassails.
But ever and ever their voices shrill
Proclaimed Alaska an iceberg still.
And such is the power of pen and tongue,

Such is the range of a bellowing lung,
That all the wide world took freely for granted
The slanderous legends these raucous ones ranted.

In time, as the placers of gold were drained,
The adventurers fled, and the strong remained.
They wrested a living yard by yard
 From the forests dense and the northwind hard.
To prove with their days of toil and stress
That this land they loved was no wilderness.
Until at long last Uncle Sam grew jealous.
His fostering care waxed over-zealous.
And Alaska was thwarted by endless debate.
While her hopes were strangled in crimson tape
Amid the congressional laws and acts
Based on pet theories instead of facts.

It took all the lessons in living she'd learned,
And all of the loyal devotion she'd earned
For this primordial land of the midnight sun
To say to her Uncle, "I'm twenty-one!"

Written for the pageant,
"In this Place,"
Alaska Day, October18,1959

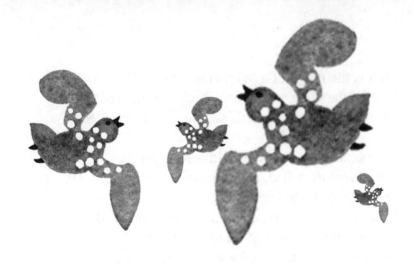

GLOSSARY of ALASKANISMS

Baleen: A plastic-like material that hangs in strips from the upper jaw of a baleen whale. They act as a sieve through which the whale filters krill, plankton and other small organisms of the sea that are its nourishment. Baleen whales are the Blue, Bowhead, Gray, Humpback, Minke, and Right. This substance, made of keratin like fingernails, is used to weave beautiful water proof baskets. It is glossy and black.

Bearded seal: Large arctic seal with tufts of long whiskers on each side of muzzle. It is highly prized for both meat and hide.

Cache: An elevated storage cabin used to keep meat and other foodstuffs away from prowling animals.

Cheechako: A newcomer to Alaska.

Dog Salmon: Any salmon except King, such as silvers, humpback, and chum, that would sell elsewhere for dollars a pound, but here are considered suitable to be dried for dog food.

Eskimo Ice Cream: Crisco shortening or seal fat mixed with any kind of local berries and frozen.

Fancies: Decorated borders for parkas and mukluks. Often marvelous works of art.

Ice worms: An old Alaskan joke perpetrated for many years by bartenders who put pieces of limp spaghetti into drinks and told tourists they were ice worms. Curiously enough it turns out there actually are ice worms.

Mukluks: Boots made by Eskimos. Comes from the Yupik name for bearded seal because an Eskimo man when asked what his boots were called thought the question was what were they made of and replied with the animal's name.

Muktuk: An Eskimo delicacy. The outer whale skin with blubber attached. Eaten raw. It is dark gray shading to pink shading to white and looks a little like a common coconut candy.

Oogruk: Inuit name for bearded seal. Its most commonly used name.

Outside: Term used for the "lower 48" states. A person from the states is therefore an Outsider.

Parky: Northern Alaska way to pronounce parka.

Permafrost: Permanently frozen ground beneath the surface soil that thaws. In spring.

Sourdough: An old-timer in Alaska. Comes from the fermented dough used by prospectors who didn't have yeast.

Trash dog: Any breed of dog that isn't used to pull sleds. You don't see many cats in the far North.

Tundra: The swampy, lichen-covered plants that cover most of the interior of northern Alaska.

Ulu: Native fish knife with half-round blade.

Willawaw: An Aleutian storm characterized by mini tornado-like whirlwinds especially treacherous on the water.

SUGGESTED

READINGS

Buchan, L. and Allen J. *Hearth in the Snow*. New York: Wilfred Funk, 1952.

Johnshoy, J. Walter. *Apaurak in Alaska*: Dorrance & Co., 1944.

Larsen, Helge and Rainey Froelich. *Ipuitak and the Arctic Whale Hunting Culture*. New York: Anthropological Papers of the American Museum of Natural History, Vol. 42, 1948.

Muñoz, Juan. *Cliff Dwellers of the Bering Sea*. National Geographic Magazine, Vol. CV, No.1, January 1954.

Senungetuk, Vivian and Paul Tiulana. *A Place for Winter*. Anchorage Ak: CIRI Foundation, 1987.

Service, Robert. "The Shooting of Dan McGrew." *The Best of Robert Service*. Blaine WA: Hancock House Publishers, 2004.

Toynbee, Arnold, *The Study of History*. Taken from the Abridgement of Volumes 1-V1 by D.C. Somervell. New York: Oxford University Press, 1947.

INDEX

Adak 33, 209
Akutan 20, 55, 56,57, **71***, 206
Alaska Airlines 198
Alaska Coastal Airlines 39, 68, 190, 198
ACCA 21
Alaska Native Brotherhood 40
Alaska Native Claims Settlement Act (ANCSA) 200
Alaska Native Service (ANS) 16,18,27, 28, 30,32-36, 48, 102, 110-1,138-9,
Alaska Steamship Co. 18
Denali 18, 23-29, **68**
Flemish Knot. 148,154, 160,163
Amchitka 209
Anasazi 200
Anchorage 199, 209
Anderson, Mr. & Mrs. 164
Annette Island 24
Antarctic 109, 173-4
Anuruk, Mrs. 165
Apaurak (see Brevig, Toleef)
Arctic Circle 13, 98, 106-6, 115-6, 131, 146
Arguella, Maria Conception 10
Athabascan 19, 24
Attu 209
Baranof, Alexander. 10, 36, 37
Baranof Castle 36-7
Baranof Elementary School **69**
Baranof Island 41
Bartletts 160, 208
Bay of Naples. 198
Belkovski 54-55
Benzell, Mr. 101
Bethel 34,128, 167, 213
Besboro Is. 167
Bishop, Mr. (Mate) 161
Blatchford, Charlie **81**, 162
Joe **81**, 162

Mama **81**, 161-3,166, 170, 184, 187-90
Violet **81**, 162, 178
Boxer 186
Boxer Bay 166, 186, 191
Breidig, Carolyn 97,114, 207
Brevig, Toleef 155-60
Bristol Bay 46,187
Buchan, Laura 45-48
Bureau of Indian Affairs (BIA) 15, 198
Burg, Amos 53, 128-9, 164, 173, 207
Burton Island, USN 196
Byrd, Adm. 17, 109, 173-4
Cape Douglas 198
Cape Lisburne 127.147-8,168
Cape Prince of Wales 155
Catholic Church 177
Fr. Tom (King Island) 177-8
CIRI Foundation 199
Civil Aeronautics Assoc. (CAA) 24,25, 31, 33
Civil Air Patrol (CAP) 125
Clam Gulch 191
Cole, Cecil C. (Moe) 17,107-109,161, 169-70, 187, 194, 196
Connally, Miss 115,120
Darby, Roger (Sparks) 59, 161, 167, 194-5, 213
Deering **84**, 122, 154
Diomedes (see Little Diomede)
Dogs 57, 113-4, 126, 135, 177
Pixie 19-20, 26-9, 41-2
Dutch Harbor 52, 56, 57, **71**, 187-8, 205-8
Dykes, Mr. 122
Elephant Point 198
Elim 20, **83**, 163, 168-71, 208, 210,
Elton, Mr. 56-58

*****Boldface** type refers to illustration or photograph

Fairbanks 144, 209
Ferguson, Archie 111-112,115-6, 124-5,163
Fish River 64, 99, 100,
Gaddie, Nurse 53, 98, 110, 135, 138,161, 187
Garfield, Viola 25, 28
Gastineau Channel 27
Goddard Hot Springs 41-43
Googe, Dr. and Mrs. 27, 211, 213
Golovin 63, 64, 98, 99,151-2, 160-1, 161-4, 207, 208-9
Gulf of Alaska. 52-3, 190-1, 205
Haggerty, Emma (Willoya) 157-9
Haida 200
Hanson, Mrs 127-8
Hanson's Hotel 113-114, 129
Homer 162, 190
Hoonah 39
Hooper Bay 58, 59, **71**, 160, 205, 208
Hovick, Marcia Gambrell 203
Ivy, Hazel 16, 53, 54, 61, 96, 102, 107, 127-30, 195-7, 206-7
Jackson, Sheldon 137
Japonski Island 29, 31
Jette, Miss (Pub.Health nurse) 164
Johnson, Grandma & Grandpa 145
Juneau 26-28, 34, 176, 193, 208
Baranof Hotel 28
Kanankanak 34
Kenai Peninsula 189
Ketchikan 25, 26
King Cove Cannery 55
King, Mr. (Mate) 54,108
King Island 15, **86-93**, 155,172-83 185, 198-200, 209, 213
Ukivok Village, 176, 181, 200
Kivalina 20, 98, 143,149-51
Kobuk **73**, 116,123,126,131, 168
Kodiak Is. 189
Kodiak 38, 46, 188-9
Kotzebue 13, 34, **74-5**, 103, 106, 131, 135, 154, 148,160, 201-3
Hospital **74**, 112, 115, 121, 123, 126, 182, 201

Maniilaq Association 201-2
Krowels (teachers) 134
Kruzof Is. 31
Kuskokuim River. 167
Lapland 137
Laplanders 156,164
Larsen, Dr. & Mrs. Helge 122,127-8,146
Lion's Club 40, 209
Little Diomede Island 15, 105, 116-122, 155, 174, 180, 182-5
Maisonville, Dr. 139
Maori 200
Mekoryuk 20,160, 208
Metlakatla 24, 25, 208
Moore, Dr. Philip 112, 195-6
Morgan, Stanley 142, 173
Mountain Village 208
Mutt, Willie 62
Mt. Edgecumbe Community 31-36, 48,52,143, 184, 188, 190, 198, 208
Mt. McKinley 24,111, 205
Sidney Lawrence painting 28
Mukluk Telegraph 125-6
Muñoz, Juan 181
Muñoz, Rie 181
National Geographic 53, 181
Nelson Is. (see Tanunak) 160
Nome 160, 172, 175, 198, 208
Norton Sound 60, 63, 104, 146, 153, 160, 163, 208
Nunivak Is. (see Mekoryuk) 160
Olivet College, MI 204
Okpeah, Clare 142
Osmer, Fran & Per 190
Ossorgin, Fr. Michael 38-40, 107
Ousinki 189, 209
Penrod, Max 209
Pavlov Volcano 54, 206
Post, Wiley 141-2, 173
Petersburg 26, 27
Pettitt, Mr., and Mrs. 97, 101,151
Pt. Barrow 15, 34, **77**, 138-42, 203
Pt. Hope **78-9**, 116,143,147-8
Ipuitak Site 122, 146-7

Whalebone Cemetery **78-9**
Pt. Lay 20, **76, 80**, 125-6, 143-5, 153
Rabeau, Dr. 111-112
Rainey, Prof. Froelich 146
Ramsay, Robert 204
Reindeer 103, 137-8,155-6,158-60,
Resurrection Bay 190
Rogers, Will 141-2, 173
Russia (USSR) 183, 209
  Big Diomede Is. 183-2
  Moscow 39
Russian Influence 60
  On California. 10
  Bishop Innocent 37
  Borokovsky, Vladimir 37
  Father Sergius 37
  Orthodox Church 36
  Russian-Alaska Fur co. 37
Russians 124
San Antonio, Texas 185
Salenjus, C.H, Capt. (Skipper)
  17, 58,97, 103, 104,107-9,
  123,131,138,142,161,163,166,
  191, 195-6
Savoonga (see St, Lawrence Is.)
Seattle. 17,18, 23, 26, 48, 193
  Harborview Hospital 127
Service, Robert 56
Seward 26, 188, 162, 190
Sherman, Dr. Mary 16, 53, 54, 63,
  81, 96, 102, 111, 127-30, 135, 140,
  169, 185, 193, 195-6, 209, 212
Shuler, Barbara Rose 9, **96**, 192-3
Shuler, Mark 9
Shuler, Robert H. PhD, MD,
  (Bob) 15, 18, 30, 48, 49,127,
  167, 208, 211-3
Shumagin Islands 54
Shishmareff 131,154
Shaktoolik 165, 167, 208
Siberia 16,150, 155, 187
Simmons, Miss 140
Sitka 9, 17, 18, 23-44, 52, **66-9**,
  188-9,191, 193, 197-8
  Shore boats 36, 49, 198
Skin boat **76**, **84-5**, 116-120, 193

Sprattling, William 185
St. Lawrence Is. 15, 185-7
St. Michael 60-63, 208
St. Michael's Cathedral 36-38, 61,
  66-7, 69
Sundt, Sig 104,106-107, 121, 123,
  130, 142, 166, 186, 195, 210
Swedish Covenant Church. 164,
  210
Taku Glacier 27
Talcott, Miss 101
Tanana 34
Tanunak 208
Teller Mission 104,153,155-60,208
Thomas, Austin 150
Tiulana, Paul 198-9
Tlingit 200
Toina, Edgar 125-6
Tommy 104,166
Toynbee, Arnold 6
Tsar Alexander 10, 37
Tuberculosis 11,139-40
Umiak (see skin boat)
Unalakleet *80, 82,* 163-5, 167,
  173, 208, 210
Unalaska 52, 207-8
Unimak Pass 52
Univ. of Alaska 184
Univ. of Washington 168, 185
U. Of W. Press 25
US Navy 30-3, 138-9
Vassar 209
Wales 98,154, 198
Wainwright 126-7, 132-5,138.144
Wanzer Bill, 97,
  103,110,117,123,151-2, 167
White Mountain School 16, 33,
  61, *72*, **97**, 101, 104,151,161
Whooping cough 135
Wiens Alaska Air 114-115, 120
Willoya, William 199
Wilson, Mr. & Mrs. 122-3,
Wrangell Narrows 26, 27
Wrangell 33
Yupik 21

More g...
Hanc... ...ers

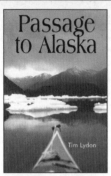

Passage to Alaska
Tim Lydon
ISBN: 0-88839-523-X
SC, 8.5" X 5.5", 243 pp.

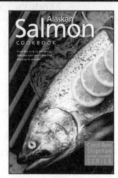

Alaskan Salmon Cookbook
Carol Ann Shipman
ISBN: 0-88839-583-3
SC, 8.5" X 5.5", 96 pp.

Alaskan Berries Cookbook
Carol Ann Shipman
ISBN: 0-88839-582-5
SC, 8.5" X 5.5", 96 pp.

Tlingit: Their Art and Culture
David Hancock
ISBN: 0-88839-530-2
SC, 8.5" X 5.5", 96 pp.

Tlingit: Their Art, Culture and Legends
Dan and Nan Kaiper
ISBN: 0-88839-010-6
SC, 8.5" X 5.5", 96 pp.

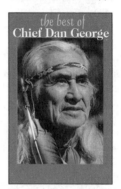

Best of Chief Dan George
Chief Dan George, Helmut Hirnschall
ISBN: 0-88839-544-2
SC, 8.5" X 5.5", 128 pp.

Alaska Calls
Virginia Neeley
ISBN: 0-88839-970-7
SC, 8.5" X 5.5", 208 pp.

Best of Robert Service
Robert Service
ISBN: 0-88839-545-0
SC, 8.5" X 5.5", 128 pp.

Broken Wings
Gregory Liefer
ISBN: 0-88839-524-8
SC, 8.5" X 5.5", 304 pp.